Poetry About You

Ronnie Brackett

outskirtspress
DENVER, COLORADO

The opinions expressed in this manuscript are solely the opinions of the author and do not represent the opinions or thoughts of the publisher. The author has represented and warranted full ownership and/or legal right to publish all the materials in this book.

Poetry About You
All Rights Reserved.
Copyright © 2015 Ronnie Brackett
v4.0

All rights reserved solely by the author. The author guarantees all contents are original and do not infringe upon the legal rights of any other person or work. No part of this book may be reproduced in any form without the permission of the author. The views expressed in this book are not necessarily those of the publisher.

Unless otherwise indicated, Bible quotations are taken from The King James Version.

Cover Photo © 2015 thinkstockphotos.com. All rights reserved - used with permission.

This book may not be reproduced, transmitted, or stored in whole or in part by any means, including graphic, electronic, or mechanical without the express written consent of the publisher except in the case of brief quotations embodied in critical articles and reviews.

Outskirts Press, Inc.
http://www.outskirtspress.com

Paperback ISBN: 978-1-4787-4111-4
Hardback ISBN: 978-1-4787-4262-3

Outskirts Press and the "OP" logo are trademarks belonging to Outskirts Press, Inc.

PRINTED IN THE UNITED STATES OF AMERICA

Acknowledgements

There are many people, instances, and situations that have inspired the writing of the poems, songs, and stories in this book—from the new love I had in high school to the many adventures I have had through life's journey.

I am blessed to have my children, so many friends, and family members who bring inspiration to my writings.

To my wife, Diane, whose understanding helps keep me on track. She spent many, many hours aiding me in finalizing this book. For her, I have written many poems and songs. She is "My Diamond."

Contents

Acknowledgements..iii
Introduction xi

This is a Book About...
Yourself xv

A Poem For You When

You think about your life…
Another Day.. 3
I Am the Only One 4
In Death.. 5
Life Today 6
Melancholy Time 8
Moments Shared... 9
My Cage.. 10
My Reflection... 11
On Stage 12
Only Mine 13
Peaceful Time 14
Perfect Moments.. 15
Quitting Time 16
Surely They Would Come 17
The Joy of You... 20
The Wind 22
Treasured Moments 23
Words Spoken 24
Yourself 25

A Poem For You When

You're looking for new love...

Fear of Love	29
Finding Her	30
Finding Him	31
In My Dreams	32
Searching	33

A Poem For You When

You've found a new love...

A Rose	37
Cherish the Thought	38
Dating the Waitress	40
Just for You	41
Just Loving	42
Love That's Real	43
More Than a Friend	44
My Diamond	45
My Pearl	46
Our Tree	47
Sharing Time	48
Stopping Time	49
The Need of Us	50
Young Love	51
You're Real	52

A Poem For You When

You've found true love...

Better Times	55
Diamond in You	56

Friends	57
Love for Eternity	58
Love Words	59
Loving You Loving Me	60
Moments Shared	61
My Angel's Touch	62
My Love	63
Only Ours	64
Perfect Moments with You	65
She Loves Me	66
Touching My Valentine	67
Your Man	68

A Poem For You When

You've lost someone…

Alone Again	71
Flower in the Wind	72
For a While	73
Goodbye Best Friend	74
Holding You	75
I Tried	76
Loneliness	77
My Mother Keeps Me Warm	78
My Old Horse	80
You Have My Heart	82

A Poem For You When

You remember an old love…

A Place of Memories	85
A Story in Your Book	87

Book of Special Memories 88
Box of Memories 89
Chapters in My Book... 90
It's Been a While... 91
Remember When 92
Stories in Our Book... 94
The Other Side 96

A Poem For You When

*You think about different things…
sometimes silly…mostly true…*

A Rhyme.. 101
Dead Boys Rising.. 102
Glory Lost... 104
I'm Drivin' My Tractor to Work...................... 106
Life... 108
Life's Circle 111
Reaching Out 112
Spring 113
The Old Apple Tree 114
There It Goes 116
To the Waitress 117
Wasting Time 118

A Poem For You When

You feel God is on your mind…

Believing in Me Again 121
Born Again.. 122
I Live On... 123
My Morning Star.. 124

My Prayer	125
No Fear in Death	126
Our Words Our Prayers	127
The Best In Us	128
The Best Things	129
The Comfort	130
The Lot of Man	131
The Waves of Life	132
What You See	133
Writing Me a Letter	134

Short Story and Things to Think About...

The Better Bull	137
Improving Happiness	143
Your Best You	145
Attitude	148

Songs...Copyrighted, Written, and Recorded by

Ronnie Brackett (ronniebrackett.com)

A Father's Love	152
Cloud Nine	154
Cowboy Cody	155
E-Mail	156
Everlasting Love	158
For the Fallen	160
Heaven On Earth	162
I Think of Yesterday	164
In My Dreams	166
It's Been a While	168
Little Things	170
Lost Soldiers in the Sky	172

Loving You With Country Songs	174
Make It Last	176
More Than a Friend	178
Not Through Loving You Yet	180
Reunion	182
Revelation	184
She's My Lady	186
She's Precious	187
Sittin' On My Porch Swing	188
Tell Me	190
The Love Bug Itch	192
The Love of My Life	194
We're Still a Family	196
Where Roses Bloom	198
Write a Song for Me	200
You're Real	202

Summary for You 205

Introduction

If the scent from a flower lifts your heart,
If the grasp of a baby's hand around your finger
Gives your life total meaning,
When you've lost it all and someone holds you close,
And you feel you have everything,
...That's Poetry

As you are reading these poems, stories, and notes

BE NOT IN A HURRY!

These words are for your heart, your memories, new loves, old loves, and forever love. These poems will awaken old memories and feelings that you may have forgotten. Some will make you smile. Some will touch you in various other ways—

LET THEM TOUCH YOU!

Some poems will speak louder to you than others. You will find a poem that will have an impact on your life and may touch that inner being in you. Take time to find that poem you feel was written just for you. Copy and hang it in a picture frame where you will read it again and again.

ENJOY READING YOUR STORY

No one will read the same poem and receive the same meaning as you. It will bring out feelings from your life's experiences, so let this poetry surround you for all the uniqueness that you are.

Cherish the feelings.

It is *you* that makes your poem so special.

Ronnie believes—"We write our own book of life; it is up to us to make our book worth reading."

This book is
"Poetry and Songs About You"

THIS IS A BOOK ABOUT...

Yourself

You look at all your yesterdays,
Memories gone forever,
The journeys that you've traveled,
They're yours, forget them never.

You write the words of your past,
With each minute passing,
Pages in your 'book of life,'
'Memories,' it's asking.

Not always sure which way to go,
But everyday's a lesson,
A lesson called 'experience,'
With hope, you keep on guessing.

You look back on yesterday—
Journeys where you've been,
You read this book of who you are,
So you'll remember when.

Always changing, as you grow,
It's yours, so live it well,
You write this book of who you are,
This book is called, 'Yourself.'

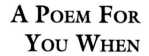

A Poem For You When

You think
about your life...

Another Day

My senses tell me where I am,
To bring me back to life,
I've been in a 'never' land,
O, most of the night.

The sunlight beckons me with warmth,
I know he's telling me,
It's time to move the day ahead,
To touch, to feel, to see!

The band of sounds they start to play,
The usual tune they know,
It's time to live another day,
Come on! Get up! Let's go!

So much to see, so much to learn,
I wish to do new things,
I'll fill my life with all I can,
Much more to life I'll bring.

So out of bed, I push myself,
Awake and on my way,
My body moves, not very well,
To live another day.

I Am the Only One

I know I am somebody,
Whose value is my own,
Though I'm different from the world,
With me, I'm never alone.

Unique in all my thinking,
Unmastered are all my plans,
I'm first to do what I've wanted,
I'm not like other men.

My mother had no other,
The time that she had me,
She raised me, not like my brothers,
They were much different you see.

I'm first to see life's journey,
Through the lens of my eyes,
No one 'thinks' like I do,
Or feels my laugh, or cry.

I only, write my story,
Experience the things I've done,
I know I am somebody,
And I am the only one.

In Death

If ever there was sunshine,
If ever there was rain,
If only I could see the snow,
Or feel the heat again.

To see the flowers, to smell the breeze,
The fresh cut grass and sky,
To laugh, to hurt, with someone else,
If only I could cry.

I did not know to cherish these,
Little delights of life,
My focus was on other things,
I did not see the light.

Now my life, it is not there,
My feelings, they are not,
For I am just lying here,
In death I am caught.

*No matter the circumstances of your life,
live it to the fullest with enthusiasm and thankfulness.*

Life Today

Yesterday is gone forever,
Tomorrow is only a vision,
Today is all we have, you see,
'Now' is the time for living.

Live for today and fill it with joy,
It gives our future some hope,
Tomorrow's memories of yesterday,
We live them now you know.

Find today, the best in things,
It is the time of your life,
Experience all varieties,
Cherish the loves you try.

Find beauty in every moment,
Enthusiastically live,
Bless your life's extensions,
Love with all you can give.

Today we'll live forever,
Until the morrow shall dawn,
Then 'now' will never be again,
We'll only live it once.

Remember your dreams of yesterday,
Live for tomorrow with hope,
Most of all, live life today,
'Now' is the memory you'll know.

Yesterday's gone forever,
Tomorrow is only a vision,
Today, is all we have, you see,
'Now' is our time for living.

Melancholy Time

I take a moment in the night,
>I want to make it rhyme,
>This, I need for me right now,
>>A melancholy time.

My days are filled with busy things.
>Peaceful times are few,
>So I take this hour for me,
>>In focus, life renews.

I hide away in my world,
>Alone in my own bliss,
>Because this time is only mine,
>>I need this little rest.

I take this journey everyday,
>To search the things I feel,
>In solemn mind I say a prayer,
>>For wisdom that is real.

Tomorrow, I'll go on with this life,
>Realizing nothing's mine.
>Except these moments when I live,
>>This melancholy time.

Moments Shared

I've been a friend and lover,
Some enemies I've had,
Sometimes I hurt with laughter,
Other times I'm sad.

This moment that I share with you,
Feel me through my words,
Let them soothe both our lives,
With meanings we've assured.

I write my life with poetry,
My songs I love to sing,
To touch someone's feelings,
My words mean everything.

I give to you a treasure,
A moment we both feel,
Sharing, touching, learning,
That's how my life is real.

So little time in my world,
To live, to love, to care,
I am so glad I can write,
About our moments shared.

My Cage

My days go by,
I take no time,
To see what is in me.

I cage myself,
Lock up my heart,
Not to touch or see.

Expressions,
Of lonely thoughts,
I keep deep inside.

No chance I take,
To share my heart,
I am alone in life.

With all my wanting,
To be touched,
I hide under my cover.

I chain myself,
Within myself,
Alone, I have no other.

My Reflection

While looking in the mirror,
Who's looking back at me?
Is that how I view myself?
Does my reflection see?

I climb into that mirror,
To see the other side,
Now I'm looking deeper,
At me, myself, and I.

Outside, you'll see little flaws,
Inside, I have a few,
I hide them from the world you see,
Oh, if they only knew!

I have a conversation,
Talking to myself,
What I see is vanity,
I really need some help!

I mirror this reflection,
Inside, much more I see,
I'm the only one who knows
The real image of me.

On Stage

My dreams,
        They are so much to me,
                I carry them around.

They live,
        They breathe, they fill my time,
                They lift me when I'm down.

In faith,
        I only play the parts,
                Of how my dreams should be.

I see,
        I have the leading role,
                To play the 'part' of me.

I build,
        The character of myself,
                In every possible way.

I feel,
        People are watching me,
                As an actor on my stage.

Only Mine

With my brush,
I color life,
The best as I know how.

With my song,
I make life rhyme,
The notes are playing now.

With my pen,
I write more scenes,
The parts that I must play.

With my breath,
I seek out life,
The joy from day to day.

With my thoughts,
I've memories,
The blessed days and nights.

With my words,
I show the world,
The picture of my life.

Peaceful Time

The turmoil of this life I have,
With deadlines everyday,
I watch the clock, I work so hard,
No time for 'me,' I say.

My days are rushed, so fast they go,
And peaceful times are few,
I must live this time right now,
I'll make this moment new.

I sit and watch the stars tonight,
Escaping for a time,
A little peace for me right now,
This evening, I'll make mine.

Others passing by I know,
Don't feel my 'little bliss,'
What I have is only mine,
Right now I feel my best.

I close my eyes and smile inside,
I'm happy as can be,
My world right now, it seems so right,
A peaceful time for me.

Perfect Moments

Life will never be perfect,
Sometimes we stumble and fall,
The crazy things we say or do,
If we could…erase them all.

Sometimes life seems empty,
All vanity it seems,
How are we truly happy,
Never fulfilling our dreams?

But then there are some moments,
We keep in our 'memory file,'
Cherished memories we have,
These moments make life worthwhile.

Do you remember your first kiss,
Or when your baby was born?
All of life was perfect then,
When those perfect moments form.

When something makes you laugh,
Cherish that moment in time,
That's when life's worth living,
Like poetry and rhyme.

When life seems down and dreary,
And happy times are few,
Remember all the many,
Perfect moments in you.

Quitting Time

Is there ever a quitting time,
        A place to get away?
    Where time forgets the toils of life,
        These long and tedious days.

Where never there'll be a stress at all,
        Of who is wrong or right?
    No work or even chores to do,
        No one to argue or fight.

To get away from the world,
        No nagging worries at all,
    Where you cannot be bothered again,
        No one will ever call.

Yes, there is a way to quit,
        "Never again!" you'll cry,
    A time for you to find some peace,
        You'll find it when you die.

…Are you ready to quit?

Surely They Would Come

The old man was up before the sun,
He made his bed, and straightened up,
With care, he put on his very best clothes,
He hoped the day was warm,
For this was a 'special' day,
His eyes welcomed the dawn,
He would wait for his children,
Surely they would come.

Not caring to eat his breakfast,
He just wanted to sing,
He would have plenty to eat,
With all the food they would bring,
Such joyful, youthful, happiness,
Such energy in the air,
His kids and grandchildren,
Soon would all be here,
To talk about 'old times,'
Will be, 'so much fun,'
On the front porch he waited,
Surely they would come.

His stomach started growling,
It was close to noon,
So he enjoyed some noodle soup,
With his favorite spoon,
"Something has delayed them,"
As he sighed a deep one,
Longing to see his children,
Surely they would come.

He didn't take his daily walk,
Like he usually does,
Nor visit with the neighbors,
That, he really loves.
He dared not take his daily nap,
To rest his weary soul,
He wanted to be awake in time,
To meet them at the door,
The house was clean as a whistle,
His chores were all done,
On the front porch, waiting for them,
Surely they would come.

His children don't live far away,
But seldom, they come by,
For they are all married,
With their own lives,
So he understands why.
But 'today' is a 'special day,'
Although, it's almost done,
"They will be here,
They know the way,"
Surely they would come.

He lit a fire in his stove,
For it was often cold at night,
And put a candle in the window,
So they could see the light,
His supper was small,
Didn't eat it all,
His head was tired as it was,
He didn't undress, as his bed was undone,
He wanted to be ready,
Surely they would come.

He kissed the picture, by the bed,
His wife of 60 years,
"I'll be seeing you soon," he said,
His eyes filled with tears,
"You're with me on my birthday,"
The old man was eighty one,
As he closed his eyes, he said it again,
"Surely they would come."

The Joy of You

We are eternal travelers on a cosmic journey
Stardust
Swirling and dancing
In the whirlpools of infinity

Life is eternal
Expressions of life are momentary and transient
As passing summer clouds
Or as lightning strikes
A flash of brilliance for a moment
And then it is gone

In this brief moment
Of our lives
We touched, we shared, and we loved
We must cherish this precious moment
Because it is transient
Only a 'wink' in our eternity

We must be sure the times that we share
Are filled with caring and love
To create an abundance of joy for each other
And in doing so
Our precious memories
Make this moment called life
Worthwhile

In this journey of life
I am glorified
To have the precious opportunity
To touch the love of you

What we created and shared as our paths crossed
I'll always remember to be
So wonderfully beautiful
So I will carry the joy of you
With me
Forever

The Wind

Forever it blows,
Through the trees,
Just playing a song,
On the leaves.

Bringing its music,
Through the years,
By the dust of man,
His sorrows, his tears.

This wind travels mountains,
And deserts and fields,
It sees all life,
And death the earth yields.

It sees the people,
Small and great,
And laughs at their power,
Their vanity, their fate.

For they shall all die,
Into dust they'll descend,
To play songs on the leaves,
By the power of the wind.

Treasured Moments

With my poems
I color life
As best as I know how

With my words
I sing you songs
The music's playing now

We share a truth
In our lives
Treasured moments in time

I touch your heart
With these words
Read how you've touched mine

Precious are
Moments like this
Memories we'll never forget

Always know
As years go by
I'm not through loving you yet

Words Spoken

The spoken word is our master,
    Unspoken words are our slaves,
        Except the sound of our laughter,
            Be careful what we say.

Our words show what we look like,
    We're judged most every day,
        Beautiful or ugly,
            Our words make us that way.

Yourself

You look at all your yesterdays,
Memories gone forever,
The journeys that you've traveled,
They're yours, forget them never.

You write the words of your past,
With each minute passing,
Pages in your 'book of life,'
'Memories' it's asking.

Not always sure which way to go,
But everyday's a lesson,
A lesson called 'experience,'
With hope, you keep on guessing.

You look back on yesterday—
Journeys where you've been,
You read this book of who you are,
So you'll remember when.

Always changing, as you grow,
It's yours, so live it well,
You write this book of who you are,
This book is called, 'Yourself.'

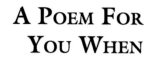

A Poem For You When

You're looking for new love...

Fear of Love

All day, all night
I think of her
The things I might say
I am for sure
That I will mean
But
I am confused
This fear of love
That I might lose
And
My heart would suffer
With feelings of guilt
That
I could have loved her
That's what I'd felt
And
So alone
I might be
If I should lose
Someone
Who could love me.

Finding Her

O where will I find her,
This joy, this love of mine?
The one that I am searching for,
I miss her all the time.

Is she in the meadows?
I'll search the mountain tops.
Or walking by the oceans?
Where I go, she's not.

I've searched the streets of cities,
The bars, the alleys too,
I've traveled 'cross the deserts,
In places old and new.

I've looked when there was sunshine,
I've walked through rain and snow,
O where will I find her?
I don't know where to go.

She's nowhere in the distance,
So vainly I have roamed,
If ever I will find her,
I'll bet she's close to home.

Now when I stop searching,
For this love I need,
Just when I'm not looking,
That's when she'll find me.

Finding Him

O where will I find him,
This joy, this love of mine?
The one that I am searching for,
I miss him all the time.

Is he in the meadows?
I'll search the mountain tops.
Or walking by the oceans?
Where I go, he's not.

I've searched the streets of cities,
The bars, the alleys too,
I've traveled 'cross the desert,
In places old and new.

I've looked when there was sunshine,
I've walked through rain and snow,
O where will I find him?
I don't know where to go.

He's nowhere in the distance,
So vainly I have roamed,
If ever I will find him,
I'll bet he's close to home.

Now when I stop searching,
For this love I need,
Just when I'm not looking,
That's when he'll find me.

In My Dreams

I think about the way she smiles,
And lays her head on my shoulder,
She then looks up to kiss my lips,
O! How I love to hold her.

The whole world seems so divine,
Sharing moments like this,
We laugh, we play, we kiss again,
In love, such wonderful bliss.

We cuddle there beneath the stars,
So happy to share this time,
I am so glad that she's with me,
Fulfilling this love of mine.

But…then I wake up from my dream,
And I cry to think that it's over,
She does not know the way I feel,
I'm only her secret lover.

Searching

Why are people the way they are?
Why do they hurt me so?
It is I, who let them,
Foolish me, I know.

I fall in love too easy,
Sometimes I love too fast,
I know, I love too many,
They never seem to last.

Always, I'll be reaching,
Hoping they'll reach back,
A lonely life, so empty,
Patience is what I lack.

In all the world of so many,
Needing to find 'love true,'
Who'll fill this empty heart of mine?
And will I fill theirs too?

Still, I'll keep on searching,
Not sure where they will be,
I need to give my love,
To someone searching for me.

A Poem For You When

You've found
a new love...

A Rose

I give to you this special rose,
I feel it's only right,
To share with you how I feel,
To be with you tonight.

Unfolding in its beauty,
Discovering parts of you,
As you open love to me,
The way you seem to do.

The softness of the peddles,
Like when I touch your skin,
You open up your beauty,
Soft fragrance in the wind.

This rose is so lovely,
Like sunshine in your heart,
Shining through your pretty eyes,
You, are a work of art.

We have so much together,
I know you feel the same,
I give to you this special rose,
Please kiss me once again.

Put this rose in a book,
And save it for all time,
So you can see it again and again,
And feel this love of mine.

Cherish the Thought

I think about our special times,
Treasures shared, of yours and mine,
Those fresh new memories of you.

Feelings of you and me,
Touching, holding...everything,
Have you cuddled with those memories too?

Did an angel touch my heart?
A constant ache when we're apart,
I miss you with warm thoughts everyday.

To feel the touch of your skin,
To laugh out loud, with you again,
I'm captured by the words that we say.

I kiss your lips, I feel you breathe,
I hold your body next to me,
I want you in my arms, all night long.

I need to feel you want me too,
These special times of me and you,
From my heart, I'm writing you this poem.

Somehow I know, I'm not a fool,
Every moment, wanting you,
Feelings so complete, with what we share.

All the times we've had before,
I'll never stop, wanting more,
Times of feeling love, and how we care.

I'll dream of holding you tonight,
With you it's good and so right,
The passion that we share is true.

You're everything in my mind,
Feel the words in my rhymes,
Cherish just the thought, I love you.

Dating the Waitress

I walked into the restaurant,
You smiled and said, "Hello,
You can come and sit right here,"
Your eyes seemed to glow.

Attracted by your pretty face,
I asked "How are you?"
We shared warmth instantly,
I know you felt it too.

I liked it when you smiled at me,
As you served my food,
Somehow you seemed to touch my heart,
You made me feel so good.

We made a date, we laughed a lot,
We shared the sweetest times,
Enjoying just the tease of love,
I asked if you'd be mine.

I smiled when I heard you say,
"You know I'm not your type,"
Then I held you in my arms,
We know it feels just right.

Dating my favorite waitress,
I know you like it too,
Everyday, we feel more sure,
Loving the things we do.

Just for You

Just for you,
I write these words,
And hope you'll understand.

Just for you,
I share myself,
I give you all I am.

                    Just for you,
                    I sing my songs,
                    Music from my heart.

                    Just for you,
                    I give my love,
                    Not sure where to start.

                                      Just for you,
                                      I have this smile,
                                      It happens when you're around.

                                      Just for you,
                                      I share this dream,
                                      Thankful for love we've found.

Just Loving

Thoughts of you throughout the day,
I always have to smile,
You feel so good in every way,
Your quality and style.

I cannot say all I feel,
With only words in a rhyme,
I really like looking at you,
To me, you are so fine.

I feel you, too, do think of me,
In ways like I do you,
It's been so nice, these last few days,
I know you like it too.

We share so much, it feels so good,
We talk, we laugh, we kiss,
It's been so long, since I've felt,
Such happiness as this.

Tonight I'll sleep and dream of you,
Dancing in my arms,
The way it was, the night we met,
Holding you so warm.

We take a chance, with love so new,
But love is what we need,
I want more of what we've found,
Just loving you and me.

Love That's Real

Exciting thoughts I have for you,
These pleasures that we feel,
The way you look into my eyes,
And ask me, "Is this real?"

I don't know, could be a dream,
Of what we see as love,
But if I am asleep right now,
I hope I don't wake up.

I'm in a place of total bliss,
Is this real, or not?
I hold you close and kiss your lips,
I never want to stop.

I'm captured by what we have,
Always thinking of you,
You are what I'm looking for,
You feel the same way too.

There's nothing solid in our life,
Except the truth we feel,
All my heart, I dare to lose,
To have a love that's real.

More Than a Friend

You're more than just a friend
I've found
To share my life
With you around
You make me laugh
I watch your eyes
A sparkle of
Sweet sunlight
You lift my heart
Throughout the day
I feel so happy
In many ways
Life's much better
When you're around
Because
You're more than just a friend
I've found.

My Diamond

The wind was hard, against my life,
A cold and lonely trail,
An uphill path of deep thick mud,
I tripped and I fell.

As I laid there in despair,
A sparkle caught my eye,
It was really out of the way,
Should I take the time?

I just could not look away,
This sparkle pulled at me,
So I walked over, curious,
And there, would you believe!

This sparkle was a diamond,
What a wonderful find!
A beautiful treasure to my eyes,
Could I claim it as mine?

In my pocket, by my heart,
I carry this treasure with me,
My spirits are high, the smile on my face,
Everybody can see.

Now life, feels easy to walk,
My way seems downhill too,
The diamond I have close to me,
Is no one else, but you.

My Pearl

There's motion all around me,
That lives and moves my life,
I close my cage and lock it,
To keep out pain and strife.

Now safe, I'm in my shelter,
Alone, I am content,
I live my life in freedom,
In darkness time is spent.

I peek outside one moment,
To touch the outside waves,
And now, there is a pebble,
It's moved into my cage.

It sees what I've been hiding,
My secretes are all known,
It starts to grow inside me,
I'll never be alone.

I feel so much better now,
To have a pearl in me,
Because it is so lonely,
Deep in this large, wide sea.

Our Tree

Let's plant a tree together,
One that's green in any weather,
One that grows toward the light of every day.

Let us cultivate the ground,
With bits of love all around,
We'll nurture all the roots by things we say.

Let's be patient as it grows,
A lot of love, a lot of hope,
We'll watch our tree get stronger in good time.

Then we'll share the sweetest fruit,
From the love of me and you,
This solid, healthy tree of yours and mine.

Sharing Time

I write for you this little poem,
Just simple words in a rhyme,
Of how I enjoyed meeting you,
And how we shared our time.

Attracted by your pretty eyes,
I sat down next to you,
We shared a warmth, it was so good,
I know, you felt it too.

There was no strangeness, none at all,
Our conversation flowed,
We felt good feelings for a while,
But then you had to go.

My heart reached out to keep you there,
For just a little longer,
You never know, we'll have to see,
Our feelings might grow stronger.

So I write you this little poem,
For you to remember when,
The time we shared, it touched my heart,
I hope to see you again.

Stopping Time

I remember holding you,
I'd touch your face, your skin,
I wrap my heart around this time,
When I 'remember when.'

So soft your voice, your pretty eyes,
I held you close and tight,
There was nowhere in this world,
I'd rather have been that night.

We watched the clouds, the rain was warm,
As lighting struck the sea!
We didn't care, we kissed again,
Time stopped for you and me.

We put our lives on hold that night,
Those moments stopped the clock,
Caressing, holding, loving you,
Memories sealed and locked.

Now when I hear the thunder roar,
Or rain touches my face,
That's when lighting strikes my heart,
These memories fall in place.

I'll cherish all we shared that night,
Forever in my mind,
When I read this poem of us,
The night that we stopped time.

The Need of Us

I met you in a lonely time,
An empty need in me,
The instant that your eyes met mine,
I wondered, could you see?

It was too late, instantly known,
'Available' was I,
But you reached out and took my hand,
I wasn't sure just why.

I felt so open to your eyes,
You read me like a book,
I did not care to close myself,
Inside, I let you look.

I let you read a part of me,
My dreams and personal thoughts,
I shared with you my deeper self,
That even I'd forgot.

Those tender parts of me you took,
And held them close to you,
So we can build a friendship here,
'Cause you might need me too.

Young Love

If I had control over inches,
I'd shorten your height to mine,
I'd make my years be older,
If I had control over time.

I think you are so pretty,
Your beautiful eyes I see,
Your smile, it wins me over,
'Cause you are just perfect to me.

In love for the first time,
Infatuation for you,
I know you are much older,
I don't know what to do!

Can I tell you my feelings?
Should I give you a kiss?
For me, I'm just dreaming,
Falling in love like this.

My dreams, hopes, and wishes,
They're all for you it seems,
I'll love you only in secret,
You are this little boy's dream.

You're Real

I can't believe how I love you,
My feelings, they are strong,
I cannot stop, I don't know why,
It seems that we belong.

And sure, I know, we've only met,
And I've had love before,
But you are real, so very real,
I want you, more and more.

I tell myself, 'stop giving in,'
Will you break my heart?
I see your eyes; they're in my mind,
And that is where it starts.

I can't believe how I love you,
That is a question still,
But, if I can keep seeing you,
I do believe I will.

A Poem For You When

You've found true love...

Better Times

I'll share with you, feelings I have,
And hope that you can see,
With time, you will understand,
My love for you and me.

Somehow you just seem to know,
When I'm feeling down,
You cheer me up and make me smile,
I love when you're around.

Things that I worry about,
They're not to worry you,
But you support in caring ways,
Loving the way you do.

Burdens seem much lighter when,
I have you by my side,
I don't feel so alone,
When I want to cry.

I love you more than you know,
Thanks for everything,
Stick with me through hard times,
Whatever times may bring.

Better times will come to us,
And we'll look back and say,
"It wasn't hard to stay with you,
And love you anyway."

Diamond in You

While walking along,
You happen to see,
A diamond on your way.

You'd grab it right up,
You'd hold it so tight,
O! What a glorious day!

You would feel,
On top of the world,
A diamond in your palm.

What a treasure,
So beautiful,
Your heart would feel so warm.

Your walk would be,
With energy,
Such joy all around.

Never would you,
Want to let go,
Of the diamond you've found.

These moments we share,
With feelings so good,
They all, with you, are true.

I treasure the time,
And love we have,
I found a diamond in you.

Friends

If I like me when you're around,
We must be friends.
A better part of my life is our time together.

We communicate in the best of ways.
We rely on a bond of understanding.
There is an acute perception of us.
I value the respect and support we have for each other.

We may not always agree, but we never condemn.
We always want to give more than we get.
Even the very best of us needs forgiveness.
It's easy to forgive you and some days, you will need to forgive me too.

Friendship makes our lives worthwhile.
We just like what binds us together.
Because…
I sure like me when you're around!

Love for Eternity

This little rhyme is a simple way,
I'll try to express how I feel,
Words from my heart, to touch your heart,
Of feelings, we know are real.

I love to write these poems for you,
And some, I'll turn into songs,
It's perfect, when you're in my arms,
That is where you belong.

Looking at you, feels good to my eyes,
Your voice is sweet to my ears,
I'm so amazed, how pretty you are,
I praise your beauty with tears.

Let's celebrate every day,
With joy, for you and me,
And know someday, when our bodies are gone,
We'll love for eternity.

To my forever love.

Love Words

I love the words that we say,
Beautiful words everyday,
Always claiming our love, you and me.

Our life's a novel, and how it shows,
Beautiful lovers, who seem to know,
How they belong and need to be.

When I read the words inside,
They are the words that I write,
About your smile, your touch, your pretty eyes.

And I know, you feel it too,
The way we fit, me and you,
You know, you are the love of my life.

I don't get tired of looking at you,
And I can feel, you're looking too,
I see it in the way your smile just shines.

As we grow from day to day,
With loving words we'll always say,
I am so pleased that you are mine.

You are the sweetest person I know,
You might get sweeter, as we grow old,
You cuddle next to me all night long.

You feel so right in my life,
Kiss me more and hold me tight,
You are the love words in this poem.

Loving You Loving Me

If I could catch a rainbow,
That's just what I would do,
I'd wrap it all around your heart,
That's what I'd give to you.

If I could build a mountain,
With flowers on all sides,
That's where we would build our home,
We'd smell sweet breeze all night.

If I could catch the brightest star,
I'd name it after you,
I see that star in your eyes,
I know you love me too.

With you I have a world just right,
With everything I need,
Holding on with all my might,
Loving you, loving me.

Moments Shared

I've been a friend and lover,
Some good times we've had,
Sometimes we hurt with laughter,
Other times, we're sad.

These moments that I share with you,
Feel me through my words,
Let them soothe both our lives,
With meanings we've assured.

I write our life with poetry,
Your songs, I love to sing,
To touch only your feelings,
Words mean everything.

I share with you a treasure,
A moment we both feel,
Giving, touching, learning,
That's how our life is real.

Let's keep these special moments,
In memories of our time,
So precious now and forever,
Moments of yours and mine.

My Angel's Touch

I feel above the world right now,
An angel walks with me,
She'll hold me close with so much love,
The finest place to be.

A spotlight seems to follow her,
Wherever she may go,
She's royal, her own majesty,
She's just the best, I know.

She sends a meaning to my life,
I feel her angel's touch,
I'm honored how she shares my life,
By loving me so much.

My Love

Someone loves me
Out of the entire world
Someone shares time with my life
I've nothing to hide
With all of my faults
True love pushes them aside
To make room
For all the love we share
This special one puts life in me
This love of mine
Understands the core of 'good' that I have
Sees my imperfections
And stands by me anyway
Is proud of me
Sees my silly side
And laughs with me
Inspires me
To be my best
And loves me more when I'm not
Comforts me
Forgives me
Believes in me
In a way that only my best is seen
That is my love

Only Ours

If I could find a wonderland,
That's just what I would do,
I'd share with you its beauty,
Such joy I feel with you.

Our fairytale would be a land,
With flowers on all sides,
That's where we would build our home,
We'll watch the stars at night.

I'd give you all the treasures,
Found in land and sea,
But all these things I'm finding,
Impossible for me.

I cannot catch a rainbow,
It's always far away,
No fairyland to give to you,
Our home is where we stay.

I'll give to you a flower,
We'll watch for falling stars,
We have all these treasures,
This love is only ours.

Perfect Moments with You

Life is sometimes unfair,
And never will be perfect…,
But sometimes we have 'perfect moments' with
    someone special,
Those 'perfect moments' make our life worth it all,
So with all of life's imperfections, and foolish
    things we've done,
Thank you for some 'perfect moments' in my
    memories of you.

She Loves Me

I have a lady,
        Of all the chances,
        And circumstances,
  Of my world...,
                She loves me.

I have a friend,
        The good she sees,
        Forgiving me,
  With all my faults...,
                She loves me.

I have a sweetheart,
        A time for us,
        To share our love,
  Those precious moments...,
                She loves me.

I have a love,
        All through the night,
        We feel so right,
  Oh how I know...,
                She loves me.

I have a woman,
        In all her beauty,
        She still tells me,
  With all her heart...,
                She loves me.

Touching My Valentine

I see our love in your eyes,
I'm captured when we touch,
I feel the warmth of every day,
By loving you so much.

I know I have touched your heart,
You know how you've touched mine,
With joy I write this poem for you,
To touch my Valentine.

Your Man

I have this 'little boy' inside,
He loves to be with you,
You make him feel so wonderful,
In all the things we do.

Inside his heart, he can tell,
The love is growing strong,
He cannot get you off his mind,
He's smiling all day long.

These words I'll rhyme to touch your heart,
I'll hope you understand,
I want to share my life with you,
This little boy's your man.

A Poem For You When

You've lost someone...

Alone Again

I'm crying here,
        In my bed,
Misery in my life.

My insides hurt,
        I try to see,
And understand why.

How, in my life,
        Of all the world,
Now, I'm so alone.

I feel so lost,
        I have no one,
The love I had is gone.

This nagging ache,
        And pain I feel,
Hurts so deep, so sharp.

I'll get by,
        Somehow I'll try,
To live with this broken heart.

I hope I'll find,
        Someone in time,
To share true love with me.

Someone who'll fill,
        These empty arms,
I'm alone again, you see.

Flower in the Wind

I am a flower in a field,
But yet I feel alone,
I am of many others,
We try to get along.

The wind does blow me all around,
And I do bow to him,
My stem must bend, I must not break,
Whichever way he sends.

It hurts sometimes to bend so low,
When he does blow so fast,
That's when he tears my peddles off,
In tears, I watch them pass.

Naked I'm left, my pride is torn,
But I must bloom again,
And hope next time, I'll have more strength,
To stand against the wind.

For a While

For a while…
You were here
And you touched me
O! For that time I lived
And yearned to reach
More toward you.

For a while…
You filled my time
With such joy
That we expressed together
And you remember.

For a while…
I felt the warmth
Of your feelings toward me
Which I accepted gladly
As my own toward you.

For a while…
We had joy together
You and me
The memory of that time
I'll remember with a smile…

For a while.

Goodbye Best Friend

You closed your eyes; I said, "goodbye,"
I held you close as you died,
My tears would not stop, I watched you go.

I'll always keep you inside me,
In my heart, those memories,
Of how you loved me, too, I know.

Those years I had with you around,
When I came home, I'd hear the sound,
Of your happy welcome at the door.

It is so sad…now you're not here,
Empty silence…I just stare,
It hurts…I won't see you anymore.

I stare at your picture again,
All the times I remember when,
You always were around to be with me.

The way you looked into my eyes,
I could feel the bond that ties,
Our hearts…so together, so complete.

Unconditional love I got,
And loving you, I'll never stop,
Remembering all the joy we shared, too.

I lay to rest my best friend,
These feelings I have, will never end,
I'll always have memories of loving you.

Holding You

If only I could hold you,
And feel your arms 'round me,
The 'wall' that was between us,
Has fallen, can't you see?

> If only I could hold you,
> And have you by my side,
> You see, I still remember,
> All those precious times.

If only I could hold you,
Memories in my mind,
Of the days we had before,
So happy all the time.

> If only I could hold you,
> That's when our world was right,
> And you would kiss me once again,
> I need you close all night.

If only I could hold you,
That's all I know to say,
My heart is still missing you,
It's hurting every day.

I Tried

I tried to call your number,
But stopped, before I could start,
I guess I couldn't show you,
This aching in my heart.

I tried to write a letter,
But didn't know what to say,
I guess it might be better,
If I would stay away.

I tried to be more patient,
And hope you'd miss me too,
My days go by, slowly now,
Because I'm missing you.

I know, it's just a poem,
But it's all I know to send,
You see, I still love you,
I'm trying to tell you again.

Loneliness

Loneliness is to me,

    A ghost that is felt,

        But, I cannot see,

            Except for these tears,

                Which are left behind,

                    For someone lost,

                        Who I thought was mine.

My Mother Keeps Me Warm

I could not go and play in the snow,
Until I was dressed by mom,
"Wear your coat, put on your gloves,
Don't be out too long."

Memories of years gone past,
I'm old and very gray,
All the 'ups and downs' of life,
I'm comforted today.
> Her love was always caring for me,
> My mother keeps me warm.

I feel the chill of a winter's night,
The cold on my arms and legs,
In the cedar chest I find,
A quilt my mother made.

Her hands worked every strand,
To weave the patterns here,
It's been packed away for years,
I forgot that it was there.
> I wrapped it around myself and thought,
> 'My mother still keeps me warm.'

With tears in my eyes, I feel her here,
Sometimes, I miss her so,
I'll always feel her love in my heart,
Somehow, I think she knows.

Her fingers touched every part,
Of this beautiful quilt you see,
She weaved her love into my heart,
I feel her touch on me.
> Even though she is not here,
>> My mother keeps me warm.

My Old Horse

I still can see those trembling legs,
The first time you would stand,
My newborn colt just stared at me,
And gently touched my hand.

The bond we felt when we were young,
You'd follow me around,
You grew so big and beautiful,
I'd ride you, O so proud.

We had so many treasured times,
Both rain and sunny days,
The things we shared so long ago,
Remain with me today.

We'd run across the grass and trails,
Those playful times we had,
Still, I see your big brown eyes,
And now…my eyes are sad.

You've carried me for many years,
So loyal you have been,
My heart will always carry you,
When I 'remember when.'

My old horse died at thirty-two,
I'm saddled with memories,
Of riding on my favorite horse,
Wonderful times for me.

I say "so long" to an old, old friend,
In tears, this is goodbye,
My heart will always ride with you,
As you gallop through the sky.

You Have My Heart

You said goodbye yesterday,
And that's okay with me,
I guess I'll do what I want,
Now that I am free.

Without you holding on to me,
I'll do so many things,
I think I'll ride a butterfly,
Or twist a dragon's wing.

I can lift, you know,
A mountain with my toe,
Or put a rope around the wind,
And never let it go.

So fast, I will forget,
Your smile and pretty hair,
The way you cuddled close to me,
And all the love we shared.

You know I'll never do these things,
I cry 'cause we're apart,
My body is away from you,
But you still have my heart.

A Poem For You When

You remember
an old love...

A Place of Memories

We have to keep the times we've shared,
In a place of memories,
They must be saved and never lost,
Those times of you and me.

I cannot praise your beauty enough,
With only words in a rhyme,
Nor can I touch your warm soft skin,
And hold it next to mine.

But in my mind, I must record,
Your laughter and your smile,
Your silky hair, your warm soft eyes,
Your own beautiful style.

The way you looked into my eyes,
As you held my hands,
The rush I felt when we kissed,
I want to feel again.

To taste your lips, to feel you breathe,
Our passion was so good,
The perfect bliss of loving you,
The way two people should.

Pretend I'm there and kiss me soft,
Then whisper out my name,
Good memories will come back to you,
And I will do the same.

Please put this poem somewhere safe,
Where you will read it again,
And treasure all the love we shared,
When you remember when.

Remember all the love we felt,
For a moment in time,
This special love that's only ours,
Memories of yours and mine.

A Story in Your Book

Raise the cover, open me,
    Words and pictures I let you see,
        The surface of what I am.

Turn my pages, read my life,
    About my days and my nights,
        You will start to understand.

I share with you my story,
    All my words, all my glory,
        In my depths, I let you look.

When you're done reading me,
    Inside you, I'll always be,
        A story in your book.

All the people we touch, or who touch us, we will find that they bind together the wholeness of our personal 'Book of Life.'

Book of Special Memories

I wrote a book 'bout you one time,
    So I'd keep you in my mind,
  On a shelf of memories of my past.

My heart will hold you once again,
    With all the love of remembering,
  Those special memories, I still have.

I wonder if you have thoughts too,
    Of the days of me and you,
  When all we gave was love, and love we took.

The times we shared were only ours,
    Tho' years have passed, seems only hours,
  When I read the pages of our book.

Again, you are on my mind,
    Touching thoughts of long, lost times,
  The feelings that we had were everything.

Those feelings, I remember still,
    And I know I always will,
  Treasure special memories you bring.

I smile when I 'remember when,'
    You touched my heart, way back then,
  I cherish those special feelings, you see.

My heart still holds a place for you,
    That's just what memories do,
  You'll always be a special lady to me.

Box of Memories

We share a box of memories,
We have the only key,
Unlock this box once in awhile,
And you'll remember me.

Hold them close to your heart,
Relive the time we had,
Happy times to make you smile,
And maybe a little sad.

Always feel the joy of love.
We shared in that time,
Hold these memories close to you,
This love of yours and mine.

Now when you put them back again,
And gently close the lid,
Kiss me again, in your mind,
Please hold me like you did.

Be sure to lock our box again,
So nothing will get out,
Seal it tight with your love,
You'll let me go for now.

Then place the key upon your heart,
That's where I need to be,
A special box of memories,
Sealed for you and me.

Chapters in My Book

There are chapters in my book,
When in the past I do look,
I find our story told.

I will read them, now and then,
So I can 'remember when,'
When I am grey and old.

Loving you, I've never quit,
Our younger days, in total bliss,
That's how love was meant to be.

Many years have come and gone,
Still, I see you in this poem,
Time's so precious for me.

My heart will never say, 'goodbye,'
I'll always love you, that is why,
With feelings that I have of younger days.

In my heart, that's where you'll be,
Cherished memories, of you and me,
And you'll be there, always.

When my book is finally written,
My last chapter, the last one given,
I'll write in your heart this truth.

You're the 'first love of my life,'
I've never felt a 'love so right,'
As the love I had with you.

It's Been a While

With thoughts of you in my mind,
Remembering our loving times,
Just memories coming back with a smile.

I call you up, we meet again,
I tremble as you let me in,
You touch my hand…it's been a while.

For a time we sit and talk,
About old times we laugh a lot,
You still have that same pretty style.

The way you move, your sweet perfume,
Could it be I still love you?
We'll have to see…it's been a while.

Seems like only yesterday,
All the lover's games we played,
When we were young and fairly wild.

I see now why I've missed you so,
My heart has never let you go,
Still loving you…it's been a while.

Remember When

Thoughts about a special night,
When everything was just right,
Still fresh in my memories of you.

    Have you heard the thunder roaring?
    Have you felt the rain drops pouring?
    Are you cuddling with memories like I do?

I miss the touch of your skin,
I want to hear your laugh again,
Feelings that I love in every way.

    This happy aching in my heart,
    I'm so sad that we're apart,
    I miss you with these yearnings every day.

To kiss your lips, to feel you breathe,
Just to hold you close to me,
I tremble with this passion in my chest.

    My heart cries, 'I'm missing you,'
    And I hope you miss me too,
    With everything I feel, 'You're the best.'

Do you think that I'm a fool?
So far away, yet wanting you,
So thankful for the time that we shared.

    A time of memories of before,
    Only memories, I want more!
    More happy times with someone who cares.

I dream of kissing you again,
The way we did, remember when?
Do you feel someday this will come true?

> How can feelings span long times?
> Just feel the words in my rhymes.
> Cherish just the thought that I love you.

Stories in Our Book

You have opened me,
I begin to let you see,
The surface of what I am.

You have stayed with me,
And in me, you believe,
You seem to understand.

You hear the words I say,
We are closer, everyday,
We seem to know what we've found.

I love to share my life with you,
Captured by the things you do,
Feelings are so good when you're around.

We share the stories of our life,
We find the words flow just right,
Deep inside, we both look.

Our words, our chapters will always be,
Sharing words of you and me,
Loving stories in our book.

The Other Side

I was over there one time,
The other side of the road,
Remembering what was lost,
To hear old stories told.

I saw flowers blooming,
I hadn't seen in so long,
The entire world was singing,
A beautiful and happy song.

My heart felt so cheerful,
Such joy so long forgot,
I stayed as time permitted,
Every moment I caught.

I knew I had to come back,
My feelings torn apart,
For there's the life I wanted,
And there I left my heart.

Back, I crossed in sadness,
This place where I can't win,
Depressive life I'm living,
I want to be free again.

In time, I'll tear this bondage,
To find new life that's there,
With gladness, I'll feel welcome,
I'll laugh and breathe fresh air.

Don't know when I'll be there,
Just soon, I've prayed and cried,
My need, it grows much deeper,
To come to the other side.

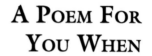

A Poem For You When

You think about
different things...
sometimes silly...
mostly true...

A Rhyme

I feel fine
In this space and time
With these lines
I rhyme
And as I climb
To go where I'll find
Some kind
Wishes of mine
That I try
Not to bind
Or make me blind
To the signs
That keeps me aligned
To a past that shines
As I look behind
In my mind…
The clock chimes
It's past nine!
I need some wine
From a good vine
I'll find a better time
For making rhymes.

Dead Boys Rising

A women's club meeting,
Only men are allowed,
Discussing all the corners,
On a table round.

Everyone was playing,
Solitary with friends,
Monday night football,
On the weekend.

We heard a bell ringing,
Someone's knocking at the door,
So we grabbed all the chairs,
And sat on the floor.

To hear a true story,
From a liar that's mute,
You've got to pay attention,
He's listening to you.

It was early in the morning,
Just before midnight,
Two dead boys rising,
Decided they would fight.

Walking with each other,
They ran in different ways,
Stumbling in darkness,
On that sunny day.

Standing back to back,
They watched each other run,
From far away, they drew their swords,
And shot each other down.

A deaf policeman,
Heard the noise,
He came and shot,
The two dead boys.

Everybody saw,
There was no one around,
Dead boys rising,
Lying on the ground.

Now if you don't believe,
That this lie is true,
You can ask the blind man,
We know he saw it too!

Glory Lost

For thousands of years,
And millions of miles,
They travel eons,
And make us smile.

They sparkle and blaze,
We pause where we are,
And watch with wonder,
We wish on a star.

There is one day,
That we celebrate,
That for this star is,
A horrible fate.

From billions of miles,
Through space it has been,
For eon's of years,
From who knows when!

O falling star,
Through night has burst,
Its glory is lost,
In the fireworks.

I'm Drivin' My Tractor to Work

No 'seat-belt' law applies to me,
No license from the DMV.
My day starts before sunrise,
A jug of water, I drink and drive.

I'll never get a ticket for goin' too fast,
Plowing this field is slow at that.
The days are long with sweat on my shirt,
But, I feel at home,
      'Cause, I'm drivin' my tractor to work.

No rush hour traffic, so I don't care,
Break lights or horns aren't used out here.
There's no road rage when you're goin' slow,
You learn lots of patience when the gear's in low.

My hat's my shade from the hot sunshine,
My air conditioner's the four season's kind.
With heavy equipment, I stay alert,
Feeling kind'a good,
      'Cause, I'm drivin' my tractor to work.

You'll never see me wearing a suit,
Dirt on my jeans and mud on my boots.
That's how I like it, I don't know why,
Just an 'overalls' kind of a guy.

My tractor's real fancy with a cruise control,
That helps out a lot on these long, long rows.
Pillow on my seat so my butt won't hurt,
Takin' life easy,
> **'Cause, I'm drivin' my tractor to work.**

I know my day's over when the sun is gone,
Supper's on the table, when the chores are done.
My family holds hands as we say a prayer,
Thanking God for all the blessings we share.

We read a little Bible, 'cause we know that's right,
We put our kids to bed, and we snuggle all night.
Another day is dawnin', I put on a clean shirt,
What a good life I'm livin',
> **'Cause, I'm drivin' my tractor to work.**

Life

There once lived in a foreign land,
Three men as blind as night,
They tried to see an elephant,
They used their hands for sight.

The first grabbed on the big beast's tail,
The second, on his leg,
The third reached up and touched its ear,
And this is what they said.

The first, who thought his knowledge true,
Proclaimed about his tail,
"An elephant is like a snake,
That sways with every gale."

"Not so!" proclaimed the second man,
"The beast is like a tree,
That plants itself upon the ground,
As solid as can be."

The third just laughed and shook his head,
"How stupid can you get?"
"An elephant is like a leaf,
The biggest ever yet!"

The argument went round and round,
Of who was right or wrong,
They all just knew that they were right,
Until a forth came 'long.

The forth, he heard the quarreling,
And went to them and said,
"What is this thing you fight about?
I'm blind. My eyes are dead."

To him they told their argument,
And then explained their views,
"So tell us, old and wiser man,
Who's right, and then do choose!"

The old man stooped and felt the ground,
Then sat upon that place,
He calmed awhile, he chose his words,
Deep thought was on his face.

"You all must take the things you feel,
And listen to your friends,
Then you, in part, will understand,
What an elephant is."

The old man left the men alone,
To think on things he'd said,
But still, they did not understand,
They fought again instead.

Believing that they each were right,
To see from no one else,
They listened not to other men,
Just focused on themselves.

But woe to them, those selfish men,
Their fate was sure to come,
For thinking that just they could see,
An elephant alone.

The first was an awful mess,
This snake relieved his bowels,
The second smashed by this tree,
So solid to the ground.

The third was swept off his feet,
And thrown against a rock,
From this leaf, there came an arm,
And in it he was caught.

They did not learn about this beast,
The danger that was there,
They all perished in the night,
Because they did not share.

The whole world lies in darkness still,
God's wisdom gives us light,
So we can share, and better see,
This elephant called 'life.'

Life's Circle

To live is to hurt,
To hurt is to care,
To care is to love,
To love is to live.

Reaching Out

With my words
I express what I feel
About my life, and what is real
O! I begin to see
That I am lost
In what I understand
About being this man
And the cost
Of living so deep
In my feelings
Which do reveal my life
In poetry
Where I keep
Feelings in my words
Which reach out
With some doubt
That my message is really heard
But still
I continue to write…

Spring

O beautiful days of promise,
Of warmth and beauty to come.
The spring! The hour that tells us,
The cold hard winter is gone.

The promise of flowers blooming,
That comes with days like these.
The grass and the trees are swaying,
In the warm sunny breeze.

Sweet songs of birds are saying,
Wake up! It's warm again.
From the cold deadness of winter,
Now, new life begins.

The Old Apple Tree

In the shade of the old apple tree,
Just brings back sweet memories to me,
I remember the time,
We were drinking our wine,
You and me.

In the shade of the old apple tree,
Sat two bums just as drunk as can be,
Said Pat to his friend,
"There's a fly on the end,
Of my nose,
Can't you see?"

Now Pat's friend was a husky old guy,
And with an axe, he went after the fly,
He smashed the fly flat,
And he buried poor Pat,
In the shade of the old apple tree.

One day I thought I'd wash off in the river,
For a bath I hadn't had in a year or two,
And for this bath I could not pay a quarter,
So I was feeling very, very blue.

I hung all my clothes on an apple tree limb,
That's when I got into an awful fix,
For an ol' maid came and sat down beside them,
She set there from one o'clock 'til six.

The mosquitoes were biting my nose,
The minnows were nibbling on my toes,

I stood there all day,
Until she went away,
From the shade of the old apple tree.

Well, me and Sue were married this morning,
They say we were the perfect bride and groom,
But some things filled my heart with sadness,
Pieces of her were scattered all over the room.

Her false teeth and glass eye were on the mantel,
Up on a nail she hung her wig of hair,
Her padded bra left nothing to desire,
Then she leaned her wooden leg against the chair.

It was a limb from the old apple tree,
And it brought back sweet memories to me,
We stayed there all night,
Our initials we'd write,
On the limb from the old apple tree.

Some people say our kids are kind of homely,
Others say they dress funny too,
I tell my wife,
"We don't need to worry,
'Cause they look just like me and you."

They spend all their time in the apple tree house,
The neighbors hear them howling all night long,
We know they drink fermented apple cider,
They're always singing good old country songs.

If ever I'm feeling kind of lonely,
I conjure up some sweet memories,
I'll just sip from my favorite jug of moonshine,
In the shade of the old apple tree.

There It Goes

Another day
Comes to an end
Never will
It be again
In this space
And time we know
Here it comes
And there it goes…

To the Waitress

I see a happy, pretty face,
Attractive friendly eyes,
Serving all a glowing smile,
I feel as she walks by.

She does not know I'm watching her,
I don't think she cares,
She sure looks nice, I must say,
I'm trying not to stare.

This good food does comfort me,
Although, I am alone,
I know I feel welcome here,
This home away from home.

A traveler's 'thanks' with poetry,
In this simple rhyme,
I hope you're smiling when I go,
I thank you for your time.

Wasting Time

Idle sitting,
        Watching a TV show,
  A world of imagination,
      No reality.

I ask myself,
        What do I find?
  Watching some other story,
      That is not mine?

Who would make,
        A show about me?
  Just sitting here?
      What would they see?

They take on the world,
        They live adventures out,
  They are heroes to my life,
      I just lie on the couch.

I never see them,
        Sitting in one place,
  Laying around like this,
      Is nothing but a waist.

My goals and my dreams,
        They will never be,
  Unless I get off the couch,
      And be a hero to me!

A Poem For You When

You feel God
is on your mind...

Believing in Me Again

In my darkness, I see Your light,
I must look up to You,
To follow in Your footsteps,
In everything I do.

I keep You out in front of me,
You pull me by Your side,
You always know what's best for me,
You've seen the things I've tried.

I feel I need to serve You,
But You keep serving me,
You push me toward a higher ground,
Than I deserve to be.

Omnipotent is Your majesty,
You know where I have been,
Still, You walk beside me,
Believing in me again.

Born Again

I HATE!
        My stomach churns,
                My insides burn,
                        TOO LATE!

I DIE!
        My spirit is dead,
                I hide my head,
                        I CRY!

I HURT!
        No one seems,
                To care for me,
                        ALONE!

I SEE!
        What vanity,
                My life to be,
                        FOR SURE!

I SOUGHT!
        Love once more,
                I'm born again,
                        IN GOD.

I Live On

Sometimes I feel so lonely,
> Though I'm never alone.

> I'm tired and life gets weary,
>> This world is not my home.

I often feel so small here,
> I know I am His child.

> And when I am discouraged,
>> It's merely for a while.

To live in His spirit is,
> The only place to be.

> With all of life's burdens,
>> I know He's here with me.

Soon, I will see Him,
> When my time is done.

> In Him, I am eternal,
>> With God, I will live on.

My Morning Star

My morning star,
    Is what You are,
        You know the things I do.

You shine on me,
    To help me see,
        In You I find the truth.

Please shield me from,
    The darts of life,
        They try to pierce my soul.

This shield of faith,
    Protects me here,
        Your word, is how I know.

Now I can say,
    In every way,
        Your scripture keeps me right.

To help me find,
    My peace of mind,
        You are my guiding light.

My Prayer

I call upon You
My Father in heaven
O! That You would bless me indeed
And enlarge the borders of my life

That my integrity be with
Your guiding hand
And that You would keep me from evil
That I cause no pain

Direct me in Your word
Always
And in Your wisdom, Father
Bless me more

No Fear in Death

When our 'mortal' is putting on 'immortality,'
Then death has no sting,
God made it that way for us.

Corruption cannot inherit incorruption,
Therefore,
Death is our victory.

After a long, hard day of work,
Sleep is a welcome comfort,
So fear not death,
Welcome eternal joy.

Reference from:
1 Corinthians 15:50-57

Our Words Our Prayers

Treasures are given to us,
By our words and our prayers,
Sometimes we cannot see these gifts,
Be assured, they are there.

We claim these blessings by what we say,
With intentions from our heart,
Whatever you say, say it with love,
Words can tear us apart.

Grow accustomed to speaking with God,
By every word we say,
We live and breathe, all by His will,
His love gives us this day.

Soon we will see, the blessings we have,
Come from the words of our past,
He listens close to what we say,
Be careful of what we ask.

Inside we carry the power of God,
In us, His kingdom lives,
With every word, we command,
The power of God within.

The Best In Us

We seek out excellence,
Every single day,
To use only the best of us,
God built us that way.

We've no excuse to just exist,
In His image we are,
Knowing we must follow His course,
No matter how long or far.

Believing in the glory we share,
His chosen vessel we be,
Touching our lives all around,
By His words we see.

We live to be our best, always,
He'll be the best in us,
Seeking joy in all we do,
Everything…with God's love.

The Best Things

Surrounded by a world of things,
I focus my life, my dreams,
Creating in my mind the best made plans.

Making sure wisdom is in,
The things I say and I begin,
To realize just where I stand.

I stand to touch many lives,
Create new dreams in their minds,
They'll follow my example with their eyes.

In God's hands, my life must be,
And I know, He's wanting me,
To be His best image, in my life.

To love, to dream, to edify,
To motivate, to set goals high,
Every soul I touch, His life I'll bring.

To understand, true value is,
Through a touch or loving kiss,
The best things in life are not things.

The Comfort

Though I wander, here or there,
    I build my world, without despair,
        I think of things, I need to be,
            Trusting He will carry me.

I stumble in darkness, when I go wrong,
    I hold His hand, He leads me on,
        I know He's there, He feels my pain,
            He lifts me to my feet again.

Though I lose all, I do not fear,
    For how much longer, this death is near,
        'Cause in my spirit there will always be,
            My Father watching, to comfort me.

The Lot of Man

All men share in His bounty,
We all are part of His plan,
No matter the labor or duty,
We build the lot of man.

>To dig or cut the lumber,
>Place windows or carry stone,
>We all labor together,
>We cannot build alone.

>>We know, He's our foundation,
>>To carry the weight of our life,
>>He made us for His glory,
>>His word shows us what's right.

>>>We build His house, His family,
>>>Our home is made for the King,
>>>Only by working for Him,
>>>Do we achieve anything.

The Waves of Life

The waves of life are churning,
Their power,
Changes things,
They carry us from what we know,
We wonder what they'll bring.

Uprooting earthly foundations weak,
With faith,
We surge ahead,
Believing we will break the bond,
From burdens past and dead.

New beginnings, unsure, but good,
The unknown spirit,
Of life,
We seek new love, embrace the thought,
His words will keep us right.

Today we'll pray,
With hope, we'll go on,
We don't want,
To look behind,
Keeping our sails towards His truth,
We conquer the waves of life.

What You See

On my knees I pray my words,
Hopeful that they'll be heard,
With everything I feel.
>I will now express my heart,
>So only You can hear the part,
>Of me, it is so real.

Inside I cry, outside I laugh,
You take away my foolish mask,
So You can look inside.
>My secrets, to You I tell,
>You take and place them very well,
>I've nothing left to hide.

You look down deep inside of me,
You softly tell me what You see,
So beautifully expressed.
>Underneath this worthless mold,
>You see diamonds, rubies and gold,
>And tell me I am Your best.

I never knew those things were there,
You made me see, You made me care,
For this life that I live.
>I'm so much more, than what I knew,
>All because of knowing You,
>And the treasures that You give.

Writing Me a Letter

I'm writing a note of who I am,
And what I see in me,
I'll try to put some details here,
Of all the things I see.

I write about the best of things,
My hopes, my dreams, my goals,
I play them out in my life,
I have the leading role.

I'll push away bad characters,
And hold to the ones I need,
They'll help me see His wisdom in life,
His truth, I must read.

I'll seal this letter with the love,
That God put in my heart,
And stamp it with His character,
His words carry me far.

Daily I'll read God's part in me,
I'll treasure every word,
He tells me I'm His precious child,
All of my wishes He's heard.

I'll write His words upon my heart,
They will be my guide,
He believes I'm beautiful,
I must prove He is right.

SHORT STORY AND
THINGS TO THINK ABOUT...

The Better Bull

The top of the chute was not comfortable, but familiar. I looked down at the massive shoulder and neck muscles of the bull that I had drawn. 'Cliff Hanger' was a great draw and I knew he was one of the top bulls in the rodeo circuit. Even though I felt I had a great draw, I also had a little fear mixed in with my feelings. A cowboy must have a good bull to have a good ride and I wanted this gigantic creature of iron muscle to do his best bucking to try to throw me. With luck and chance working for me, I knew that I was good enough not to let him—at least for 8 seconds.

I gazed at the 12 to 14 inch horns that came out in a scary, forward and upward angle from his massive head. An artist couldn't draw a more perfect set and he carried them proudly. They were not cut or even trimmed. I gazed at the broad forehead between those deadly horns. In past rodeos, I have seen cowboys tossed like a rag doll in a tornado when they were in the way of an angry bull like this one. I have never been too badly hurt except for the time I was thrown under a bull and his rear hooves raked eight inches of skin off my back. A slightly different angle and he would have gone through me. Being hit by a bull this size would be like kissing a fast train!

Like the base of a large, old, bent oak tree, the muscular neck behind this proud bull's head was very calm and still. I could see the tension in his eyes as he gazed through the gate out into the arena. He had been in many riding chutes before, but I knew his heart was pounding hard in anticipation. He was ready.

People from miles around were here, and the bleachers were completely full and noisy. To me, the sound of the crowd was like a stream flowing down a steep, rocky mountain. I had to focus on what was going to happen in the next few minutes. Attitude is everything. I must have the right one to take on this challenge and adventure I had put myself into tonight.

Like me, the clowns paid little attention to anything outside their dangerous, and very risky, territory with the bulls. They didn't dare. I know bull riding is indeed a challenge of fate and chance, but I never had a curiosity to try a clown's daredevil job. They have to be very knowledgeable about handling bulls, as well as, healthy, alert, and quick on their feet, in their profession. A professional clown will make good money, and he deserves every penny. We riders owe them our lives many times over.

Looking back down on Cliff Hanger, I could sense his anxiousness. This bull was going to buck with all his might and I was preparing for the ride of my life. Fifty percent of the score is determined on how well the bull bucks. I didn't want to lose my entry fee on this bull. Cliff Hanger is one of the best draws I have ever had and I want to take advantage of this fact.

The first night, of this two-night rodeo, my ride was fair, but I was sloppy out of the chute. The twists and turns of the bull were sharp and quick and it surprised me to reach the 8 second buzzer. The judges confirmed my sloppy ride by giving me a score of only 66.

There were four other rider's scores that concerned me. The scores of both nights were added together to decide who won first, second, or third place. Tonight, I had to be at the top of my performance because I definitely had a better bull.

"The judges gave Joe Bixler an 84 for some very good riding," I heard the announcer say. Joe came from a family of 'rodeo.' He and his sisters, Connie and Dixie, all went to college on rodeo scholarships. His dad, Roger, team roped in his sixties, and sometimes won.

Skip was working the shoots with a cast on his ankle. In his usual job as a clown, his foot was stepped on trying to save another cowboy's life— freeing him from a rope that was wrapped around his hand. Those are the chances we all take.

After the referee checked to make sure my spurs were dull so no harm would come to Cliff Hanger, Skip reached under my bull with a hook and fed my rope around to me. I could feel the tension from Cliff Hanger when I sat down on his back. We both knew I was not wanted. As I was tightening my rope around this dangerous piece of massive muscle, a drop of sweat from the tip of my nose hit the back of my hand. The glove on my right hand was sticky with tree sap/resin, as was my bull rope. As I cinched up the rope tight on my glove, my knuckles were digging into the back of Cliff Hanger, as he breathed a short but deep one.

"Out of chute #6, our next rider, is Ronnie Brackett." I felt an icy chill run up my spine as my adrenalin was flowing with the anticipation of the next few moments. Scooting my butt up tight toward the back of my hand and leaning back, I tightened my grip with all I had in preparation for that first hard lunge out of the chute. After a deep breath, I nodded my head to signal 'go' to the gate opener, as I stuck my left hand high in the air. If my left hand ever touches anything for the next eight seconds, I will be disqualified.

Instantly, Cliff Hanger shot out of the chute like a cannon ball and with about the same force! This caused a jarring shock to every bone in my body. My grip was still good as I raked both spurs back across his shoulders as we charged out into the arena. The judges watch the bull, the hands, balance, and spurs going across the shoulders for good scoring points.

Wow! With one hand, I'm riding 2,000 pounds of mean and ugly. It's too late to change my mind. If the referee blows a whistle, this bull won't stop and he doesn't care if he kills me! Sure, this is a sport of competition, but it is also *survival!* The longest 8 seconds in the world is on the back of a bull, but…what a rush!

Spurring with twists and watching the bull's head were the only things, besides experience, that helped me stay on. Always, the first two or three seconds seem to be the hardest to adjust to the motion of the ride. A good bull will change that motion in an instant. I didn't know what to expect, but my reaction to his bucking so far was working. If you were watching television while riding in the back of a fast moving truck, on a bumpy road, with no shocks or springs, then maybe you could understand the vision I have on the back of a bull.

My grip was still pulling my butt tight to Cliff Hanger because I knew if I allowed any space between us, I could lose my control and balance. The same balance that a tight-rope walker might have in a tornado. I felt that I had passed the hardest hurtle of the ride. The thoughts of every split second were so instantaneously quick that time was, comparatively, in slow motion.

His power and agility had not thrown me off balance…yet, and I had been able to catch every hard bucking sway and maneuver with the perfect counter-maneuver. I must keep it that way for a little while longer. I was still raking my spurs across his shoulders for more points. I knew I was doing well and looking good as Cliff Hanger bucked as hard as he knew how. I had to be careful not to be too confident too soon. I could lose this ride in a split second. Even the best six or seven second rides score a 'zero.'

In the 'old rodeo days' the rides were 60 seconds! But they found out that the best bulls and broncos would start to get 'broke' and wouldn't buck as hard anymore. Good riding stock is worth a lot of money and the owners don't want that to happen. That's where they came up with the 8 second ride.

Where was that buzzer?? Did they decide to take a coffee break during my ride? Did the buzzer button malfunction? Did they start my time late?

BUZZZZZZ! Such a welcome sound! I felt so good I stayed on for an extra few bucks just for show. Then to polish off my ride, I released my grip, swung my right leg over, and landed perfectly on both feet. I knew I was hamming it up, but quickly I ran to the nearest fence and stepped through to get out of the way of Cliff Hanger who might direct that ill temper he had towards me.

Breathing hard, I couldn't help but have a big smile on my face. I felt every eye was on me as I walked down in front of the audience back toward the chutes. I could feel the eyes of the younger boys on me and remembered how I used to look up to older cowboys in a childlike worship of a hero.

"That sure was a nice ride!" said Diane, the Rodeo Queen, as she pushed aside her long, red hair and winked at me as I walked by. She has always caught my eye…and a few other cowboys too. I tipped my hat and winked right back at her.

As the spotter handed me my rope through the fence, I felt my heart skip when they announced my score. "That ride was a 94! In all my years of rodeos, that was one of the finest rides I've ever witnessed," said announcer Cody Wade. "Ronnie Brackett is the first to ride Cliff Hanger to the bell!"

Did I really ride that well? I didn't know Cliff Hanger had never been ridden to the bell! Now I was really feeling good and I know my face was showing it. I had to cherish this extraordinary moment…but be humble about it…if I could!

The scores were added for both nights and I came in second with 160. I missed first place by 2 points. Brent Berry, who won first place, came and shook my hand and congratulated me for such a good ride.

I'm 60 years old now and 'rodeo' is only youthful memories. But, I still look back and smile. One of the best memories of my life was when I rode…**the better bull.**

<u>This story is fiction</u>.
I used my own name and family members to write this 'tall tale' of me being something I never was…'a great bull rider.' Most of the bulls I rode were in high school rodeos, and I rarely made the 8 second bell.

Improving Happiness

Here are five things that come from the heart that can improve happiness:

1. **Be grateful** – Write letters of gratitude to people who have helped you in some way. If you do this, you will find a lasting increase in happiness–over weeks and even months–after implementing the habit. What's even more surprising is that, even if the letter is never delivered, you will still feel better afterwards.

2. **Be optimistic** – Practice optimistic thinking. Visualize an ideal future. For example, living with a loving and supportive partner, or finding a job that is fulfilling. Then describe the image in a journal entry. After doing this for a few weeks, you will see that <u>changes do happen</u>, as well as increased feelings of well-being. As you think, so you are. Simply be happy.

3. **Count your blessings** – Write down three good things that happen to you every week and you will feel significant boosts in your happiness. It seems the act of <u>focusing on the positive</u> helps people remember reasons to be glad. Read positive books or articles. Compare what you have to so many who have much less.

4. **Use your strengths** – Identify your greatest strengths, and then try to use these strengths in new ways. For example, someone who says they have a good sense of humor could try telling jokes to lighten up the work day or cheer up sad friends. This habit, too, seems

to heighten happiness. <u>A large portion of happiness is in our power to change our attitude.</u> Attitude is everything!

5. **Commit acts of kindness** – It turns out, helping others also helps us. Giving to churches or charities is good, but people who donate time, or who somehow assist people in need personally, report improvements in their own happiness. But the best improvement to help you is to <u>be there</u> to help or be kind to someone else. Give items that you do not need to someone who does. When someone needs your help, help them. Give of your personal time. BE THERE for them!

One day as I was eating breakfast at a local café, I noticed a young couple with a new baby sitting a few tables over. Looking out the window, it appeared they had everything they owned crammed into a little pickup and moving to a new town. I asked the waitress to put their bill on mine and not to tell them. I still smile about that memory today.

You reap what you sow. Negative or positive—
it will come back to you either way.

Your Best You

If you fill your life with purpose and direction, you will find 'your best you.' Find a goal and put it into action. Belief in yourself must have action--"...faith without works is dead..." (James 2:17-26)

Perfect your personality. Be the best in everything you do, stand for, and build in your life. Draw and seek the same in others around you. Abide with your dreams and never lose the focus of who you are. Do not ever be second best to you.

Use the creativity you have in yourself. With confidence, use that spark in you to excel. Be around people who motivate you to be your best.

Make a habit of developing self-discipline in everything you do and everywhere you are. Refine your best to be even better and take pride in it. Constantly define '**integrity**' in your life.

You will profit by enthusiasm. 'Enthusiasm' comes from the Greek word 'enthuse' which means 'having God within.' Cherish this power in you because it is like the diamond you are. By your enthusiasm, many around you will see you shine. *What you give to the world will outlive you.*

Budget your time and money. Write down your goals. Chart the year, month, week, hour...see your plan on paper. Do this today, not someday! Get excited about where you plan to be in the future by the goals you have today. When your plans have to change, make the best of it and find an even better route—*but don't quit.*

Be positive and happy. Attitude is EVERYTHING! Attitude is so important that it can overcome the stumbling blocks that may keep us down. It is more important than money, our education, our circumstances, our past failures, or successes. Attitude will overpower what other people think, say, or do. It is more important than our talents, our accomplishments, or what we look like. It will make or break a company, a church, a family, and you. We have a choice everyday regarding the attitude we embrace.

Our past is yesterday…we cannot change what we or others have done. Sometimes, we are not in control of what happens to us, but we are always in control of how we react to it. A positive attitude will help you discover how to overcome negative events. All things are temporary and will pass. Work this positive life force in you. A great example of attitude and integrity is written in the book of Job in the Bible. Read the first two and very last chapters. It will give you good insight to overcoming anything that life throws at you, with the right attitude.

Remember, the best things in life, are not 'things.' No one will remember you for those things you possess, but for what you gave to the world in the moment you were here. How many hearts did you touch by the things you have said? Were you a good listener? What influence did you give to others by your examples or inspirations? The person you see in the mirror should be "your best you." You did not have the choice of when and where you were born. You did not choose your parents or other family members, but you do have a choice to be your best in any circumstance and situation throughout your life.

"You reap what you sow." What you give will come back to you multiplied! Be careful that what you give, you give in love, not hate or resentment…it will come back to you either way. What do others see you do?

The moment you were conceived, there were between 6 and 12 million sperm cells having a race toward your mother's egg…and each one of them would have created a different person. You are the result of the champion! You are a champion of millions from the moment you were conceived. Believe that, and live like the champion you are. Does a man build a powerful race car and never take it out of the garage? Is a finely bred race horse never taken out of the stall? Should you keep an eagle in a cage and never let it fly?

You were created in God's image so we are the seed of the highest majesty. It is up to you to realize that in your own life. God made only one of you for a very good reason—he didn't need two!

Attitude

Just as other people's words affect you, the words that you say to yourself also affect your attitude. Whether you feel negative or positive depends on the input that you get, including the input you give to yourself. You can't change from a negative mindset to a positive mindset without changing from negative talking to positive talking. To do that, you must change the input from negative to positive. Man is made or unmade by himself. The tools you build in your thoughts will either build you up or tear you down. Control your thoughts (Phil. 4:4-8).

Using positive affirmations is a proven technique that works miracles in many lives. Ideally, you should look yourself in the eye as you make these positive affirmations. You must start your day with a clear understanding that you control your attitude for the day. Think about the following statements every morning:

- I clearly understand that failure is an event, not a person; that yesterday really did end last night; and that success isn't final and failure isn't fatal because I only fail if I quit.

- I have the courage to admit a mistake and to say that I was wrong. I have the courage to ask for help and the courage to say "I don't know."

- I have the courage to continually strive to be the person that I am capable of becoming. Sometimes that's tough, but it's the right thing to do, and it gives me excellent preparation for tomorrow.

- I have vision in my life, which means that I see not only with my eyes but also with my heart.

- I have 1,440 minutes in every day of my life, and I will make the most of them so my 'best' can be even better.

- I am successful because I believe that to be a master of my life, I must seek humility; to recognize the need to be mentored, either in my business or personal life, by those who have greater insight, wisdom, maturity, knowledge, and skills.

- I discipline myself to do the things that I need to do when I need to do them, because I know that doing them will enable me someday to do the things I want to do when I want to do them.

- I am successful because I don't confuse activity with accomplishment.

- I must make good habits to follow in life so I have a focused purpose each day. I must not be a wanderer with no purpose.

- I recognize my mistakes. I learn from them, and then forgive myself. God forgives me, so I must not condemn myself. I must bury them.

- I am successful because I have a great sense of humor and can laugh at myself, even when mistakes are made or decisions are in error.

- I am not bothered by someone else bragging and accepting undeserved credit. I fully understand that it's not the whistle that pulls the train.

- I move forward in my life every day, even if it's only a tiny step, because I know that great things are accomplished with tiny moves, but nothing is accomplished by just standing or wishing.

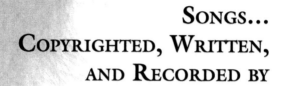

SONGS...
COPYRIGHTED, WRITTEN, AND RECORDED BY

Ronnie Brackett
(ronniebrackett.com)

To hear the music to these songs, go to Ronnie's web page and listen.
If you wish to download them, go to: cdbaby.com/artist/RonnieBrackett

Enjoy the Music

A Father's Love

You feel the greatest treasure with your baby in your arms
He touches all your feelings; you give to him your heart
It's like a touch of heaven when you watch your baby sleep
Now you understand the father's love you've had from me

It seems that we've been cheated by the way our lives have gone
We've missed some needed moments, you and I, it seems so wrong
I could not always be there like the dad I wished to be
I pray you understand the father's love you've had from me

> **CHORUS**
> Years go by so quickly since you've grown and moved away
> Sharing hugs and kisses seems like only yesterday
> So when you hold my grandson, in your heart I know you'll see
> That now you understand the father's love you've had from me

Sometimes I hope you miss me, you've moved and gone your own way
You call me for no reason; you know it makes my day
To hear my little grandson say, Grandpa, I love you
Touches me in my heart, 'cause I know he loves you too

You've grown into a good man with a path all your own
And though you don't live here, this will always be your
      home
So teach your son the best things, and with pride you
      watch him grow
Now you know what I feel of the love a father knows

Chorus

Ending
Now you understand the father's love you've had from me

Cloud Nine

CHORUS
I'm walking on cloud nine with you
I'm loving everything we do
Am I dreaming, or is our love really true
Walking on cloud nine with you.

You asked me, "Are we for real"
I am lovin' the way you make me feel
And I see the way you love me too
Walkin' on cloud nine with you.

Never dreamed a love could be as good as we are
I've never known my heart to feel this way
A fantasy to all my dreams
Our love feels so true
So I'm walking on cloud nine with you.

Chorus / Instrumental

Don't you know I never tire of looking in your eyes
I hope and pray I'm lovin' you just right
I've never known a love like ours
I know you feel it too
So I'm walking on cloud nine with you.

Chorus / Ending
Yes, I'm walking on cloud nine with you.
O, I'm walking on cloud nine with you.

Cowboy Cody

I met a young cowboy named Cody Wade
He would ride wild horses everyday
When the rodeo came into town
Cody was the best cowboy all around.

All of the other cowboys knew who he was,
Just ridin' wild horses is what he loves
Cody knew what he was doin,' you could tell
The meanest bronc' couldn't throw him before the bell.

CHORUS
Ride, ride, ride wild horses
Cody, ride, ride, ride wild horses

He'd ride those wild horses sittin' tall
They tried their best to throw him, he wouldn't fall
All the crowd would cheer him through his ride
Cody was the best cowboy of the night.

Chorus

When the ride is over, the cheerin's loud
He'll wave with a smile at the crowd
He'll ride on wild horses 'til he dies
Then he'll ride those wild horses in the sky.

Ending
Ride, ride, ride wild horses
Cody, ride, ride, ride wild horses
Come on let's ride, ride, ride wild horses
You have to ride, ride, ride wild horses.

E-Mail

CHORUS
E-mail, E-mail,
I've been searching for true love on e-mail.
E-mail, E-mail,
I just love to hear 'em say, "You've got mail."
(Female speaking) "You've got mail."

I'm out in California; you're back in Tennessee,
We fell in love on e-mail, you are my fantasy.

I hurry home from work, the first thing that I do,
Is fire up my computer, and send my love to you.

I know I chew tobacco, and I drink too much beer,
My truck is old and rusty, but you don't seem to care.

You make me feel so good, with letters from your heart,
You tell me how you're feeling, so sad that we're apart.

Chorus

The nights are gettin' longer, I miss you more each day,
Real soon we'll be together, all night, that's what I pray.

If it wasn't for my e-mail, I don't know what I'd do,
I'll send you more love letters, just to say, "I love you."

Chorus
Instrumental *(Up a full key)*

Well, I finally got to meet you and, wow, was I surprised!
Your crooked nose, your false teeth, and a pretty blue glass eye.

I tried to keep from laughing as the wind blew off your wig,
I didn't want you kicking me with your wooden leg.

Now, the only question is, "Oh will you be my wife?"
Though you're kind of homely, you brighten up my life.

We'll fill our days with laughter, and share it with our kids,
With help from my computer, I found what true love is.

Chorus (*without female speaking*)

Ending
…Oh I found my true love on e-mail …No more searching for true love on e-mail…
(Female speaking) "You've got mail!"

Everlasting Love

(Male vocal)
I remember when I held you, as you came into this world,
The joy, the precious wonder in my little baby girl.
With tears in my eyes, there was something that I knew,
I'd have everlasting love with you.

(Female vocal)
In your arms you'd hold me, whenever I would cry,
You'd fix it all with kisses; you'd make it feel just right.
Then you'd make me laugh, 'cause you'd be laughing too,
I'll have everlasting love with you.

CHORUS *(both vocals)*
As the years go by, some things will always be,
You're still that special love, always loving me.
With all my heart I live to sing this song so true,
I'll have everlasting love with you.

Bridge

(Male vocal)
I gave you at your wedding with this man you build your home,
A little house in the country, a family of your own,
And now you have a son, and I know he feels it too,
He'll give everlasting love to you.

(Female vocal)
Oh Daddy, you're my first love, I hope you'll always know.
The best things that you gave me, my heart will always hold.

(Male vocal)
From my little girl, to the woman that you grew,

(Both)
I'll have everlasting love for you.

Chorus *(two times)*

For the Fallen

I watch our flag unfurl in the sunshine,
I put my hand on my heart as we sing,
Somehow I feel that you're here with me.

I hold on to memories of your life, not long ago,
I think about the love we had, it tears my heart, you're gone I know…
That's why I feel, that you're here with me.

> **CHORUS**
> In my heart we're still a family,
> And I know, you'll always be with me,
> You gave your life to keep our nation free,
> Still you're home, here with me.

I still can see your smile as we kissed and said 'goodbye,'
Even though it's been a while, I still hurt, and that is why,
Inside I feel that you're here with me.

Without you it is so hard, and inside I'm lonely too,
You're a piece of me that's gone; I'm not complete, without you,
There's not a day that goes by, when you're not on my mind,
In memories you're still around, here with me, in my life.

Instrumental

I still hear the way you laugh; I see your smile in my mind,
The sacrifice you made, I will love you for all time,
I'll always feel that you're here with me.

Chorus

Ending
You're love will always be with me.
We're still a family,
I feel you're here with me.

Heaven On Earth

Verse 1
Did they kick you out of heaven
For wearing tight blue jeans?
You sure look like an angel to me.

Did they kick you out for walkin'
In your very sexy way?
Well you can have some heaven on Earth with me.

Verse 2
Did they send you down from heaven
Especially for me?
You're everything I've ever dreamed of.

You're such a beautiful lady,
In everything I see,
Are you my one and only true love?

CHORUS
I've never known a woman to be as beautiful as you
Your sexy eyes, you hypnotize
The way that you do.

You make me feel so good inside
I'm happy that you're here
Do you think that we could make an everlasting pair?

Verse 3
If I want to go to heaven
I'll just keep you by my side
An angel with her heart set on me.

Then we'll share our lives together
Our love we'll never hide
You're the best place for heaven on Earth to be.

Instrumental

Chorus

**Repeat verse #3
Ending**
You're the best place for heaven on Earth to be.

Instrumental

I Think of Yesterday

Mom was busy throughout the day,
She didn't have much time to play,
The little games, I asked her to.

She'd wash my clothes; she'd sew and cook,
I'd bring to her my picture book,
She'd say, later son, mama's busy, too.

> **CHORUS**
> She'd tuck me in all safe at night,
> Then tiptoe to the door,
> We'd say a prayer, turn out the light,
> I wish she'd stayed a minute more.
>
> For life is short and years rush past,
> I've grown and moved away,
> Still, I feel the love we had,
> When I think of yesterday.

My mother sent to me a poem,
Of how her nights and days are long,
With idle time and memories.

Her hands, once busy, now lie still,
The days are long and hard to fill,
She now has time to spend with me.

Chorus
Instrumental

Mom was busy throughout the day,
She didn't have much time to play,
The little games, I asked her to.

She's older now and days are long,
I'm writing her this special song,
I love you mom, I'll share this time with you.

Chorus

Ending
Still I feel the love we had,
When I think of yesterday.

Speak on end: "I love you mom."

In My Dreams

Verse 1
I think about the way she smiles,
And lays her head for a little while,
On my shoulder.

She then looks up to kiss my lips,
I brush her hair with my fingertips,
O I love her.

> **CHORUS 1**
> But then I wake up from my dream,
> I have to face what it really means,
> To be lonely.
>
> I'm off to work for another day,
> I try to push the hours away,
> They go slowly, in my dreams.

Verse 2
We cuddle there beneath the stars,
And share a love that is only ours,
O I hold her.

I tell her things that make her smile,
The happiness just seems to flow,
Before her.

> **CHORUS 2**
> I'm off to work for another day,
> I try to push the hours away,
> They go slowly.

I can't wait to get back home,
So you and me can be alone,
I'm not lonely, in my dreams.

Bridge
Repeat Verse 1 with Chorus 2

Ending
I'm not lonely, in my dreams
Just not lonely, in my dreams
I don't get lonely, in my dreams
Sure not lonely, in my dreams.

It's Been a While

I think of you from time to time,
With memories that make me smile,
I wonder if you think of me,
I hope so, it's been a while.

I call you up, we meet again,
Is there a question in your eyes?
Do you see I care for you?
I don't know, we'll have to try.

> **CHORUS**
> I wonder if we still have,
> What it takes to be friends,
> Will we forgive what's in our past?
> Will we ever love again?
>
> I wonder how you see me,
> I know I still can make you smile.
> To me you're still so beautiful,
> Even though it's been a while.

We sit and talk about old times,
We laugh about the things we've done,
The memories in our minds,
Life was mostly having fun.

Seems like only yesterday,
We shared such quality and style,
My heart has never let you go,
Even though it's been a while.

Instrumental

It feels so good to touch your hand,
And I hope you've missed me too,
Remembering the love we had,
In that time of me and you.

Let's build our love on what we are,
Only the good things we'll see.
Forget mistakes that we've made,
We'll find more love for you and me.

Chorus
Ending
To me you're still so beautiful, even though it's been a while.

Little Things

It's the little things we do,
Makes me love loving you,
Just the little things, they make life so sweet.

All our world seems so right,
Holding you close at night,
It's the little things, so wonderful to me.

The way you comb your pretty hair,
The way you walk I have to stare,
I'm such a happy man, 'cause you're by my side.

You're so beautiful to me,
People stare I'm sure they see,
I'm so proud of you, our love feels so right.

CHORUS
The pleasures of my heart, seem all to be with you,
You're everything I've hoped for; I know you feel it too.
You're my reason for living; you're the love life in me,
This song that I'm singing, it's for you, can't you see…

It's the little things we do,
Makes me love loving you,
Love the little things,
        That's how life should be.

Instrumental

We're so alive every day,
The way we laugh, the way we play,
The way you look at me, with love in your heart.

I'm so glad I found you,
In your eyes you feel it too,
And I pray to God, that we'll never part.

Feels so good we're not alone
We make our house, a happy home.
When you're close to me, you always have a smile.

Then you put your hands in mine,
I see the love in your eyes,
Just the little things, they make life worthwhile.

Chorus

Ending
Love the little things, that's how life should be.

Lost Soldiers in the Sky

Verse 1
I'm looking back in history, for those who died for me,
So many lives were sacrificed, still fresh in memories,
I open up my cedar chest, I'm looking back in time,
My helmet and my worn out boots, this 'Purple Heart' of mine.

Verse 2
I'm holding on to memories, when war was all I knew,
When fighting for my country, was what I had to do,
Soldiers that lost their lives, in a land so far away,
To keep our freedom here at home, we must still fight today.

> **CHORUS 1**
> We will fight for you, so you can stay free; we're those lost soldiers in the sky.

Verse 3
We were walking through the jungle, our shirts all soaked with sweat,
Our enemy is out there, we're gonna find them yet,
Then all at once a bomb goes off, and the bullets start to fly,
We watched some soldiers falling down; we still hear their mournful cry.

> **CHORUS 2**
> We will die for you, so you can live free; we're those lost soldiers in the sky.
> *Repeat 2 more times at the end*

Verse 4
We know our time is coming, when death will call our name,
We'll fly to soldier's heaven; again we'll see their face,
We're gonna fight forevermore; we're thunder in the sky,
We're souls who've made the sacrifice; and you'll hear our victory cry…

Repeat Both Choruses

Loving You With Country Songs

CHORUS 1
I can't climb the highest mountain,
Or swim the deepest sea,
No money for a mansion,
To buy your love for me.

With my heart I sing these words,
I know I'm not wrong,
To love you like I do with country songs.

I'm drivin' my ol' pickup,
Dressed up in my blue jeans,
A flower from the neighbor's yard,
For the girl of my dreams.

She smiles as I read to her,
A poem that I wrote,
She'll kiss me, oh how I love her so....but...

CHORUS 2
Those little things you do, the laughter that we share,
I have found everything, just knowin' how you care,
Our riches aren't with money, our treasures are so sweet,
Seems we have all we need just lovin' you and me.

Instrumental

I know my greatest treasure,
Is in your heart of gold,
You're the love of my life,
That never will grow old.

This song that I sing for you,
Is only a start,
To show you…how much you're in my heart.
…but

Chorus 1

Ending
…Oh, I love you… like I do with country songs.

Make It Last

I met you in a lonely time,
The instant that your eyes met mine, I knew.
So I asked you for a dance,
I thought I'd try a little romance on you.

You reached out and touched my hand,
I really didn't understand just why,
You treated me oh so nice,
And then we kissed once or twice goodnight.

> **PRE-CHORUS**
> And then you said, don't go too fast,
> We'll take it slow and make it last.

> **CHORUS**
> I think about those special times, when I think of you,
> Touching, holding, everything that we dare to do.
> And when I think of you and all the happiness we share,
> In my heart I hope I've found someone who really cares.

I like the way you smile at me,
The way you play, the way you tease my heart,
But I want to know for sure,
You only think of me when we're apart.

I miss the touch of your skin,
I want to hear you laugh again, with me.
And I sure like holding you,
With all the things we like to do and see.

Pre-chorus and chorus

Ending
I met you in a lonely time,
The instant that your eyes met mine, I knew.
Now you're more than just a friend,
A lot more time I plan to spend with you.
Then we say, don't go too fast,
We'll take it slow and make it last.
We'll take it slow and make it last.

More Than a Friend

You're more than just a friend I've found,
To share my life with you around, my friend,
You brighten up my day.

I have to smile when I see your eyes,
You fill the room with much sunlight,
In oh, oh, so many ways.

>**CHORUS**
>So now this poem I'll sing for you,
>I bring to you a song,
>You try to sing along…this is your song.

Instrumental

This is your song.

In harmony with you I'm bound,
I sure like me, when you're around, my friend,
You see my better self.

This happiness I feel in me,
Is like priceless gold,
Because you see a friend,
And that's my greatest wealth.

Chorus and add:
This is your song,
This is your song.

Not Through Loving You Yet

CHORUS
I'm just not through lovin' you yet,
My eyes are still seein' the love that we have,
My arms are wide open,
My heart won't forget,
I'm just not through lovin' you yet.

The moment I met you,
My heart came alive,
Your warmth and your beauty,
The way you hypnotize.

I cherish the moments we've shared in our lives,
I'll not find another,
Our love feels so right,

'Cause…**Chorus**

You think our love might fade,
And someday grow old,
The warmth that we share,
Could somehow get cold.

As long as the sun shines,
My heart will stay true,
When the stars all fall down,
I'll still be lovin' you.
'Cause…**Chorus**
Instrumental

I want you by my side for the rest of my life,
I've never known a love that feels so right.
These feelings that I have are forever, you see,
I'll never get tired of you loving me.
Cause…**Chorus**

Ending
My arms are wide open,
My heart won't forget,
I'm just not through lovin' you yet.

Reunion

There's a full moon on the mountain,
I can see the winter snow,
But the blaze of the fire keeps me warm.
As I'm staring out the window,
With my woman by my side,
I feel such peace, Lord, with my family all at home,
Such sweet peace, Lord; let me keep it when I'm gone.

Watching kids laugh and giggle,
There's a joy that fills the room,
And I smile just to see how much they've grown.
O! My brother's home on leave now,
I haven't seen him in awhile,
Such sweet peace, Lord, with my family all at home,
I feel such peace, Lord; let me keep it when I'm gone.

> **CHORUS**
> Oh, it feels like home again, just the way it should,
> With mom and dad and all us kids, singing old time songs,
> Oh, brothers, we've all been away too long,
> And grandma, she just smiles a 'welcome home.'

Well, I feel a touch of heaven,
As I watch the children sleep,
And I smile, 'cause I love them more and more.
Then I snuggle next to mama, while we watch the fire burn,
Such sweet peace, Lord, with my family all at home,
I feel such peace, Lord; let me keep it when I'm gone.

Repeat Chorus

Ending
There's a full moon on the mountain,
I'm coming home…

Revelation

CHORUS
What do you think my brother,
Oh what do you think my friend,
When our Father gets discouraged,
And calls it to an end?

What do you think my sister,
And all you boys and girls,
When God decides to call it,
The end of the world?

Verse 1
We all know He's coming,
His word gives us a clue,
Everyone will see Him,
Judging me and you.

We read it in the Bible,
In the twinkling of an eye,
Now's the only time we have,
To straighten up our lives.
So… **Chorus**

Verse 2
We're gonna live forever,
But where will it be?
Is God with you discouraged?
I know he is with me.

With open arms He calls us,
He knows where we've been,

When He locks the gates of heaven,
Will you be with him?
So... **Chorus**

Instrumental

Repeat Verse 1 and Chorus

Repeat Chorus

Ending
Is your spirit ready
For the end of the world?

She's My Lady

I was captured the first time that I saw her,
How she touched me, as we danced, it felt so right,
And the first time that we kissed it was heaven,
O! We both knew it was true love from the start.

She tells me I'm her knight in shining armor,
And she'll stay by my side forevermore,
The home that we build will be what we are,
All the riches that we have will be our love.

> **CHORUS**
> 'Cause, she's my lady,
> She's everything in my life I feel love should be,
> She's my lady,
> From all the things that I am, she's the better part of me.

She dresses up, sometimes, just to tease me,
She knows she's beautiful in my eyes,
Those little things she does just to please me,
I'm so proud to have this woman by my side.

Our kids have all left home, now she's a grandma,
And you know she's still sexy in my eyes,
When I kiss her, I'm still touching heaven,
The greatest treasure in my life is *Diane* (her).

Chorus
Ending
She's my lady.
From all the things that I am, she's the better part of me.

She's Precious

I'll kiss her in the morning,
As she wakes up in my arms,
The sunshine's always brighter in her eyes.
Every time I hold her,
I know her love's for me,
She's precious, I feel, because she's mine.

> **CHORUS**
> I touch her with my music,
> I write my songs for her,
> She inspires the melodies I sing,
> But never will I find the words,
> That say how she's my world,
> She's precious, the way she touches me.

Adoring all the woman,
A class that's all her own,
So complete in life she makes me feel.
The happiness around her,
The passion of our love,
She's precious; I know her love's for real.

Chorus

Sittin' On My Porch Swing

I'm sittin' on my porch swing, talkin' to memories,
Thinkin' about the lives I've known, and what they'd say to me.

> **CHORUS 1**
> I know they'd share the joy I've found,
> I just wish they were still around,
> In my heart, they're still here with me,
> Sittin' on my porch swing.

Sometimes I miss my grandpa, and my favorite uncle's gone,
My brother died way too young…his smile, I still see.

Chorus 1

> **CHORUS 2**
> I have memories, of days gone by,
> Precious memories, they stay alive…here on my porch swing.

Instrumental

I'm holding on to memories…I feel them sittin' here with me,
Those special souls who've passed away, they're here…on my swing.

Chorus 1

Chorus 2

Ending
Sittin' on my porch swing, talkin' to memories, …they're still here with me
Sittin' on my porch swing…

Tell Me

Tell me all the reasons that you care for me,
All the joys we love to share and see,
With our lives together.

Help me to understand my love for you,
To help me see that you are true to me,
With love we'll have forever.

> **CHORUS**
> You're beautiful, so many ways,
> My words just can't describe,
> You're in my mind all through the day,
> And I hold you close at night.
>
> I love to share my life with you,
> And grow together more,
> I know that you'll love me too,
> Much more than before.

Fill me with the love we both need.
I'm loving you loving me, everyday,
In our own simple way.

Instrumental

Touch me, with the nourishment of love,
Help me reach the stars above, every way,
With love we'll have forever.

Hold me with your arms and your eyes,
You have to share this special time with me,
I'll only share with you.

Chorus

Kiss me with the passion I desire,
You like to set my heart afire, yes you do,
With our love so true,
With our love so true.

The Love Bug Itch

MAIN CHORUS
When the love bug bites, you don't know where to scratch,
You just keep a itch'n 'til the eggs begin to hatch,
He makes the old feel young, the poor feel rich,
We did a little thing called the love bug itch.

Verse 1
One day I took my baby, and I set her on my knee,
Along came the love bug, and took a bite of me,
We made the old feel young, the poor feel rich,
We did a little thing called the love bug itch.

FIRST CHORUS
Just an itty bitty bug, he goes everywhere,
No season matters to him.
And you'll never, never know, 'til he gets to you,
That's when the itch'n begins.
(**To main chorus**)

Verse 2
Some people think I'm crazy, scratching all the time,
They don't need to worry, I'm really feeling fine,
I make the old feel young, the poor feel rich,
I do a little thing called the love bug itch.

Verse 3
Life seems a little better, when you've got to scratch,
I never want to stop, so the itch keeps coming back,
I make the old feel young, the poor feel rich,
I do a little thing called the love bug itch.

SECOND CHORUS
All the boys and the girls, all over the world,
Just a itch'n for something to do,
Just give out a smile, and after a while,
The love bug itch is on you.
(To main chorus)

Verse 4
So if you're feeling lonely, I'll tell you what to do,
Just give me a hug and you'll start itch'n too,
We'll make the old feel young, the poor feel rich,
We'll do a little thing called the love bug itch.

THIRD CHORUS
Don't matter where you live, if you're young or you're old,
No matter if you're rich or you're poor,
He'll get to you, no matter what you do,
He goes all over the world.
(To main chorus)

The Love of My Life

CHORUS
You are the love of my life,
We're feeling so right together.
For you, I write my love song,
Of how we'll belong forever.

I want to sing my songs for you,
I see in your eyes you need me to,
You are to me, the best, I feel,
Is this true love? It feels so real.
Cause… **Chorus**

It feels so good when I'm in your arms,
I love your beauty with passion so warm,
In all of my life, I'll never find,
Wonderful feelings like yours and mine.
Cause… **Chorus**

Instrumental

The stars, in heaven forever we'll hear,
Songs I'm singing, of love we share,
The best of me, it feels so right
Loving each moment, holding you tight,
Cause… **Chorus**

Ending
For you I sing my love songs,
To the stars, you and me, forever.

We're Still a Family

I hear the rain drops fall on my window,
I put another log on the fire for you,
And I pretend that you're here with me.

We snuggle on the old bean bag as we watch the fire glow,
We talk and dream of days to come, the love we have, it really shows.
And I pretend that you're here with me.

CHORUS
In my heart we're still a family,
And I know, you need to be with me,
You're coming back, we'll play some games again,
In our home here with me.

It's been a year or so, your mom left with someone else.
It put a hole in my heart, without you kids, I don't do well.
And I pretend that you're here with me.

To be alone is so hard, and I hope you miss me too.
You're a piece of me that's gone, I feel complete, when I'm with you,
There's not a day that goes by, when you're not on my mind,
I want to see you laugh and play, here with me, it's only right.

Instrumental

I still hear the way you laugh, everyday, all day long,
I tuck you into bed at night, I tell you stories, I sing you
	songs,
And I pretend that you're here with me.

Chorus

Ending
You're coming back to be with me.

Where Roses Bloom

Beautiful the day and the way we met,
Such quality in you I'll not forget,
We touched each other's heart,
With a love that needs to start,
Where the roses bloom,
It was me and you.

We went for a ride one late afternoon,
You showed me a park where the roses bloom,
In poetry we talked,
Hand in hand as we walked,
Where the roses bloom,
It was me and you.

> **CHORUS**
> You reminded me of what I have missed,
> The simple joy of spring, in the way we kissed,
> And when you held my hand,
> You made me feel the man I am,
> You took me where roses bloom…

We talked about our lives and it felt so good,
To see you smile at me, like I hoped you would.
In poetry we talked,
Hand in hand as we walked,
We touched each other's hearts,
With a love that needs to start,
Where the roses bloom,
It was me and you.
<u>Chorus</u>
<u>Ending</u>
You took me where roses bloom…

Write a Song for Me

One day I was writin' a new song,
My little girl was listenin' and trying to sing along,
She put down her color book and climbed up on my knee,
She said, daddy, won't you write a song for me?

I'm always writing songs about pretty girls,
You'll hear them on the radio all over the world,
But there's a special lady, for whom I love to sing,
She said, daddy, won't you write a song for me?

> **FIRST CHORUS**
> Daddy won't you write a song for me?
> Make it sound so pretty the whole world will sing,
> Tell me I'm the best girl in your whole wide world,
> Oh, daddy, won't you write a song for me?

My little girl is growin' every day,
She's the light of my eye, in every single way,
But there's a special place in my memory,
She said, daddy, won't you write a song for me?

> **SECOND CHORUS**
> Daddy, won't you write me a country song?
> With a rhyme and a rhythm, everyone will sing along,
> You know my love for you will always be,
> So, daddy, won't you write a song for me.

Instrumental

I hope someday my little girl will know,
She's beautiful to me, oh how I love her so,
Pretty as a flower, and that is plain to see,
She says, daddy, won't you write a song for me?

Repeat first and second choruses

Ending
Please, daddy, won't you write a song for me?

You're Real

I can't believe how I love you,
My feelings, they are strong,
I cannot stop, I don't know why,
It seems that you belong.

And sure I know, we've only met,
And I've had love before,
But you are real, so very real,
I want you, more and more.

> **FIRST CHORUS**
> You're real, for me,
> You're real, for me,
> You're real, so real,
> Love is all I can see.

I tell myself, stop giving in,
I know you'll break my heart,
I see your eyes, they're in my mind,
And that is where it starts.

> **SECOND CHORUS**
> You're real, so real,
> You're real for me,
> You're real, so real,
> Love is all I can see.

Instrumental

I can't believe how I love you,
That is a question still,
But if I can keep seeing you,
I do believe I will.

THIRD CHORUS
You're real for me,
So real for me,
You're real so real,
Love is all I can see.

Repeat third chorus

SUMMARY FOR YOU

This may be the last page of this book,
but the poetry in "your" book of life never ends!

*"We write our own book of life; it is up to us to make
our book worth reading."*
~ *Ronnie Brackett*

CPSIA information can be obtained at www.ICGtesting.com
Printed in the USA
LVOW08*2142211214

419872LV00002B/21/P